How to Be a Great First-Time Father

HOW·TO·FAMILY SERIES

How to Be a Great First-Time Father

William Lehmann, Ph.D.

How to Family Series

How to Be a Great First-Time Father
How to Be Together on Sunday Morning
How to Enjoy a Healthy Family
   (Even in Stressful Times)

Unless otherwise noted, Scripture quotations are taken from THE HOLY BIBLE, NEW INTERNATIONAL VERSION®. Copyright © 1973, 1978, 1984 by the International Bible Society. Used by permission of Zondervan Publishing House. All rights reserved.

The "NIV" and "New International Version" trademarks are registered in the United States Patent and Trademark Office by the International Bible Society. Use of either trademark requires the permission of the International Bible Society.

Copyright © 1995 Concordia Publishing House
3558 S. Jefferson Avenue, St. Louis, MO 63118-3968
Manufactured in the United States of America

All rights reserved. No part of this publication may be reproduced, stored in a retrieval system, or transmitted, in any form or by any means, electronic, mechanical, photocopying, recording, or otherwise, without the prior written permission of Concordia Publishing House.

Library of Congress Cataloging-in-Publication Data.

Lehmann, William, , 1926–
    How to be a great first-time father / William Lehmann.
       p.   cm.
    ISBN 0-570-046920-0
    1. Fathers —Religious life.   2. Christian life.   I. Title.
BV4846.L44 1995
248.8'421—dc20   94-23748

---

1 2 3 4 5 6 7 8 9 10   04 03 02 01 00 99 98 97 96 95

CONTENTS

As You Begin ...   9

1. After the Initial Terror   11

   The greatest gift ... Take time to ponder ... The privilege of fatherhood ... Your child's first environment ... Dealing with morning sickness ... Helping out around the house ... Living with the moods ... Communicating with your unborn child ... Setting a routine ... The importance of your voice ... Undeserved blessings

2. Postpartum Papa   22

   Taking care of mother and baby ... Feeding your child ... Your infant's developing personality ... Making it through the night ... Reestablishing intimacy with your wife ... The first bath

3. Living Water   32

   Called by name ... Family worship with your child

4. Nurturing Your Child's Awareness of God   38

   Acceptance ... Identity ... Communication ... Habituating ... Protection

5. Nurturing a Socialized Child of God   49

Moral sensitivity ... Obeying ... Sharing ... Contributing ... Supporting ... Socializing

6. Nurturing a Cultured Child of God   61

Organizing ... Informing ... Developing values ... Creating traditions ... Sexuality ... Caring

7. "Saint" Father   78

Who is God? ... Father as role model ... Spiritual instruction in your home ... Developing spiritual habits

8. Now I Lay Me   85

The bedtime conspiracy ... Nightmares ... The child alarm clock

9. It's Not Always a Picnic   89

Father as judge ... Don't let sin grow ... Your child's "first" sin ... God's word to fathers ... When your child says "I'm sorry" ... When you need to say "I'm sorry" ... Presenting a united front

10. When to Buy the Bike   100

Protecting your child ... Keeping up with your child ... Your child's first wheels ... "First-bike" decisions

11. The Art of Cheerleading   108

Fostering family enjoyment ... Rejoicing in your differences ... Treasuring the moments

12. Father, Ph.D.   113

Parents as educators ... What's the question? ... How did you do that? ... What does God expect of me? ... Formal education

13. Assistant *Alter Ego*   119

Molding your child's conscience ... Being your child's conscience ... Ironing out the discrepancies ... Family confession

14. When All of You Are Hurting   126

Surviving childhood illness ...Taking the fear out of the word hospital *... When your child pushes you away ...*

15. A Father's Father   132

The grandfather's duties ... Listening at Grandpa's knee ... Putting time to good use ... The family network

16. The Bottom Line   137

Adding up the financial cost ... Adding up the emotional and spiritual cost ... The reality of fatherhood

As You Begin...

Most wives, when they enter upon their first pregnancy, ransack the bookstore looking for every help they can find. Husbands often act as though pregnancy is their wives' business. Nine months will give plenty of time to get ready for the responsibilities of fatherhood. As a result, books like this are usually purchased by pregnant wives and thrust into their husbands' hands with the terse instruction, "Read it!" A pregnant wife must be humored, so, curious to discover what she has purchased, he reads about fatherhood.

Fatherhood can be the greatest and most satisfying experience of your lifetime, or the worst and most unhappy, depending on how you live it. I will take you through all of a father's life, from conception through grandfatherhood. You'll discover fatherhood stretches to the end of life and, if done well, reaches even beyond the grave in the form of blessed memories.

This book has only one message: God has singled you out to be the father of someone who is forever going to be His child. You have the opportunity and privilege to help your child prepare for your joint destinies as heirs of our heavenly Father. You will never have a greater responsibility or a more satisfying task.

For obvious reasons, your child will often appear in the text as "it," English possessing no word that means "he/she." I am painfully aware of this unsatisfactory neutral pronoun. I beg that you think of "it" as though it were _____. Fill that space with the name or image you have already begun to associate with your child.

AFTER THE INITIAL TERROR

Few of life's experiences compel the complete terror a prospective bridegroom feels shortly before his wedding. The feeling has been compared to that of standing blindfolded before a firing squad. Close to that feeling must be the terror that strikes soon after your happy spouse informs you that the two of you are going to be parents. For her it is fulfillment; for you it is new responsibility that will last to the very end of your earthly existence. No more freedom!

No one prepares us males for that moment. Each one of us faces fatherhood on his own.

For too many expectant fathers, the news of pregnancy is reported outside of a marital union. One's "significant other" has suddenly gotten more significant and significantly more "other." She is suddenly a stranger who is about to burden us with something we didn't expect to face. Why wasn't she careful? Did she forget her pills? Can't she count? Why did she have to spoil this very convenient togetherness arrangement?

For most of us who get the pregnancy news within the bonds of marriage, there is much the same response. Unless you and your wife have tried for many years without success to have a child of your own, you are just as likely as other males to feel put upon by your spouse's thoughtlessness in getting pregnant. This male response is irrational, but it happens.

The early months and years of matrimony are so idyllic for most of us that we greet an intrusion of another life with mixed feelings. Added to the limitation upon our freedom, the intrusion brings added expense and often, at least for a while, one less paycheck to cover the costs. Belt tightening lies ahead. We share our anxieties all too frequently with our wife in a most undiplomatic fashion. Her radiant happiness quickly turns to sorrow, then fear. Are we going to leave her now, in her neediest time?

The Greatest Gift

But let's look at this situation from a better perspective. Your wife is about to give you, the man she loves, the greatest present a woman can give a man. But this business of pregnancy is at best an inequitable business. You both share the fun of conception. Your wife has all the discomfort and danger afterwards; you get off easy with little responsibility until your child's birth. It's only fair that you make up to her in whatever way you can for what she is sacrificing for you and your unborn child.

Once your fear begins to subside, a chivalrous feeling begins to emerge. You become protective. Unless your wife sits down immediately and elevates her feet, that unborn baby is going to leak out all over the floor, and she will collapse. Don't laugh! It will happen.

Take Time to Ponder

My wife may disagree, but my best memory of that first pregnancy, and a few others thereafter, was of how calm and self-assured my wife was when she told me we were going to be parents. She stopped off after work to verify her first pregnancy, then came home on the El from downtown Chicago to tell me. On the way home she planned the entire pregnancy. When she arrived home, she had a list of things for us to do and items to buy.

I was ecstatic with excitement, wild with joy, more insanely in love with her than ever before; she was calmly trying to decide whether we could afford a diaper service or whether she should buy a supply of cloth diapers. (Obviously, this was before Pampers). My mother settled the matter by bringing us a supply of her old diapers. Her dad started us out with several months of diaper service.

Your wife will enrich your life and, at the same time, humble you with her wisdom. Luke tells us that "Mary kept all these things and pondered them in her heart." There is a part of your wife's spiritual life she will never share with you, no matter how close you have become: those hours spent communing with God about her unborn child, pondering. With incredible mystery, the center of her earthly being shifts from you to her unborn child. Her thoughts turn inward. She, who formerly paid attention to your every utterance, now sometimes does not seem to notice that you are there. She interrupts your most passionate addresses to feel the fluttering of an inner life. She smiles a Madonna smile, proud—not to bear the Son of God—but to bear one who in time will be by Baptism a brother or sister to that Son. She, no less than Mary, is the handmaiden of the Lord.

We are humbled, if we have any manhood, silently observing how the gift of life comes into the world, born of a courageous woman. She is never better as a woman or as a human being than when she brings her child into the world, no matter what those who trumpet the cause of liberated feminity may say.

The Privilege of Fatherhood

I do not understand how any man could abandon the woman who carries his child. As her spouse, he could have the privilege to watch her as she nurtures it within herself. He is privileged to care for her, to fund her needs, and to share with her the unborn presence until he can hold it in his arms. He can be at her bedside, holding her hand in humble respect, as she gives birth.

The father who runs away from responsibility does not begin to know his loss. He does not begin to sense how his wife's heart is torn. He has left something of himself inside her that her nature and faith compel her to love, even though she is no longer allowed to love the one who left it there. She will bear her most precious gift alone. There will be no one standing there to take it from her arms and love it with her, or love her because of it.

Your Child's First Environment

Our attention in this book focuses on our children, not our wives. I assume you know how to treat your wife, how to love and reverence her as God's gift to you even as she loves and reverences you. Some of the matters I will bring up and some of the approaches I will suggest may seem to be taking your wife for granted or using her as a means rather than as a person worthy of respect. For purposes of this chapter she is an environment, the first environment in which your child will live. If you are going to care for your child during the pregnancy, it will be through your wife. If you are going to communicate with your child, it must be through her body until your child leaves it.

Your child needs a serene, orderly environment—serenity that it may develop undisturbed and order that it may be prepared to enter an organized world. Your responsibility as husband and father consists in keeping your wife as happy and serene as you can.

Dealing with Morning Sickness

Your wife will naturally focus on her condition. Morning sickness will force her to do that, if nothing else does. Women—just like men—can be disagreeable when they don't feel well. Your wife may express regret that she is pregnant. She may bemoan what she is giving up. She may cry a great deal, often with no apparent reason. During these months of pregnancy, you earn your right to be a father as you endure her criticisms, bite your lip, soothe and comfort the woman you married, and coax a smile to her lips when she is low.

Helping Out around the House

Your wife, who never showed any signs of weakness, collapses when she gets home from work and sobs uncontrollably for 10 minutes, then calmly gets up to prepare supper. During the pregnancy, you need to assume some of the home responsibilities your wife formerly bore. Continue to do them at least for the duration of her pregnancy and into the postnatal period. If you can manage it, a meal prepared by you, waiting on a candlelit table, can compensate for the difficult day she had at work. A spontaneous hug, an unexpected expression of heartfelt affection, a backrub, or foot massage work wonders to make your wife's early pregnancy bearable.

Living with the Moods

In many respects you become a sort of therapist, anticipating and identifying your wife's moods so that you can, if necessary, intercept and change them. And she will be moody. All sorts of chemicals are pouring into her bloodstream as she converts to the maternal mode of existence. Your child is draining her bloodstream of what it needs and pumping in poisons. She is both a food factory and a sanitation system. You have to keep her calm and relaxed so her body can perform both these tasks successfully.

As her waist disappears, her belly swells, and she begins to waddle like a duck, even if she never before has exhibited any vanity, your wife will break down in tears because she looks so ugly. She will doubt her feminity, suspect that you no longer love her, perhaps even imagine that you are going to dump her for a younger, more beautiful woman.

You must reassure her that she is as beautiful as ever. You don't have to lie; she will be. If she sees your love for her shining in your eyes, an inner light will brighten her face, give a magical sheen to her skin, and lighten her carriage even in the last, most heavy days of her pregnancy. She will be a splendid sight for your child's first gaze after birth.

As we prepare for retirement, my wife and I have been sorting out a lifetime of old photos detailing our marriage. My daughters have commented how beautiful their mother was when she was pregnant. Maybe our children don't tend to associate their mother with female beauty. I, of course, knew it all the time. Blessed is the Lord who gave me a wife whose love and spirituality literally shines in her face, glows from her heart, and glistens in her eyes, especially as she held one of her infants in her arms, lovingly nursing it.

Communicating with Your Unborn Child

About the fifth month after conception, you will be able to play a more active role in your wife's pregnancy. Through your wife's abdominal wall, you will be able to feel your child begin to stir. Stirring tends to occur most frequently in the early evening, about 7 o'clock or 7:30. That early evening hour is appropriate to begin family togetherness time. Communication between you and your unborn child can begin.

Talking with your unborn child isn't as difficult as it sounds. Ask your wife to lie down, probably in the bedroom or on the living room floor—anywhere she feels comfortable. You will find it helpful, and she will find it relaxing, if she can remove any confining clothing. Ask your wife to direct your hand to where your tiny child is fluttering. Stroke it together, hand in hand, through her abdominal wall. Begin softly talking to it, addressing your child by a love name if you have chosen one. Engage in intimate conversation or softly sing to it.

What does one say to a fetus? As its capacity to hear develops over the next month, your child will respond, not to verbal content, but to voice quality and inflection. So engage in love talk with your child. Ask about its "day," how things have gone, how it is feeling. Talk to it about God's wonderful world into which it is going to come; how, by Baptism, it will become a special person—a child of God. Tell your child about its mother, what she looks like, how you feel about her.

Your conversation with your child may naturally lead to sexual intimacy with your wife, which is all to the good. Your child will unconsciously associate the sound of your loving voice with the euphoria of its mother as she enjoys your affections.

Setting a Routine

By the sixth month, your child can feel, see, hear, and remember. Its eyesight will do it little good until it is born, but its hearing is acute, and it senses touch. Best of all, it is beginning to remember. You can begin to set patterns in its life.

The wake/sleep pattern of your wife's life divides your child's existence into two parts, even as the light/dark pattern shapes our sighted days. Your wife's regular times of eating, of exercise, and of rest are creating your unborn child's life.

Your regular visits to your child each day at the same time by voice and by touch, create, after a time, an anticipation on its part. You may play music for it or softly sing to it. You may pray with it, stroking it gently. You may engage, later on, in simple games of gentle stroke and fetal kick, rub and relax—whatever you may devise. Your child will respond.

The Importance of Your Voice

No matter what else you may do, talk—always talk. The sound of your voice, amid all the other loud internal body sounds, connects to the special strokes and gentle taps your child feels from your fingertips. After birth, when your infant looks in amazement at the brilliant, fuzzy outer world, your voice—no longer muffled—and that of its mother will comfort it with the awareness that it does not enter our world a stranger. Two sounds it already knows—your voice and hers—let your child know it is loved.

Undeserved Blessings

Pregnancy is special for father and mother. My wife found my kisses for my unborn gift from her a bit ticklish as I left them there upon her skin, and she drew me up to her that she might also have her share. The love of a pregnant wife and the love for an unborn child come near the top of the list of undeserved blessings that only fathers get.

In the night as he lies awake in the darkness, holding her close, stroking her hair to drain away the aches and pains of an advancing pregnancy so that she can sleep, he would not change his place with any other man. He is going to be a father! And in that silent night, he fiercely vows to God that he will always care for this woman whom God has given him, and for their unborn child. Let any foes come near while he is there—with the might of Christ he will overcome them!

Amid such fierce thoughts, sleep overtakes his will. And just as well he sleeps. Soon, during one of those weary nights, she will urgently summon him back to wakefulness with the gentle words, "It's time!" And they will travel through the dark to their own particular Bethlehem for deliverance.

Postpartum Papa

"Hello there, little one," you whisper softly to that unfamiliar person lying in your arms in the delivery room. So tiny, so fragile, wrapped in its first blanket—the most precious burden you have ever held. No baby quite like it has ever existed; it is unique; it's yours! Somehow you can't quite fathom that. You look at its tiny fingers, its incredibly delicate fingernails.

You feel like someone has kicked you in the head. Your mind is in turmoil. There is a silly grin on your face as everyone congratulates you in the delivery room and pats you on the back. You haven't done anything; your wife did all the work. Yet you have a powerful need to go somewhere, to the nearest rooftop, on television, somewhere very public, to announce to the world that your child has been born. Then reality sets in—it's time to bring your family home.

The world today is different from the world in which I cared for my wife and children, even as that world was different from the one in which my parents raised their children. My mother, who was typical of her time, had six of her children at home. She stayed in bed for 12 days after delivery. My wife delivered in the hospital and was up and walking the day after delivery. She remained in the hospital four days. When she came home, she stayed on one floor for a week and at home for two weeks. She led a quiet, restricted life for about a month.

Now, because of medical costs, young mothers return home after a day or two. The first few days home are important for your wife. She will be weak. She will be emotional, easily given to tears. Her body will be converting back to a nonpregnant condition, which will take about one month. If your wife nurses your child, she may have initial difficulties. If your child does not nurse well, she may blame herself and suffer feelings of guilt and failure until she is successful.

In addition, a few days after your wife has returned home, she will experience a blue period—very normal but very frustrating for fathers, particularly the first time it happens. She may cry for no reason. She may express fears about parental responsibility. She may accuse you of no longer loving her; suspect you of having an affair; express guilt because she does not love your child as much as she ought to or because she is not able to satisfy your sexual needs.

Once again, you earn your spurs as a father as you accept your wife's moods, hold her close, profess your love, and shower her with affection. Suddenly, she is over it and radiantly happy as though nothing had happened. She wonders why you were so concerned about her. You grit your teeth and say nothing.

Taking Care of Mother and Baby

Your wife is no longer your child's environment, but she is still its food factory. You are responsible for making sure the factory works well. This means proper nutrition for your wife, adequate sleep and rest, a serene environment, and privacy so she can recover her physical well-being. Mother and infant are developing a lifelong relationship.

Every young mother wants to see her friends and show off her baby as soon as possible. That may not be in her best interests or that of your infant. You need to watch her condition and, if necessary, limit the visits from outsiders until your new family unit has established a healthy routine.

Every father has the primary responsibility to begin to create the second environment in which his son or daughter will spend the formative years. It begins centered upon the feeding of the infant. Its focus is the mother and child, but it includes the father in the background.

Feeding Your Child

From the very beginning, the home environment

focuses on feeding and growth—nursing, meals, feeding on the Word, gathering together in worship as a family. The family grows out of the feeding time as mother and father are together with the infant while it feeds.

Nursing provides many advantages to a mother over bottle feeding. There is constant tactile communication. The infant feels her; she feels the infant. She can stroke its cheek, let it clutch her finger in its little hand, or hold and caress one of its tiny feet. She looks closely at the child; after a few weeks it looks back. She can make noises to the infant or sing to it. It will soon begin to respond with its own noises.

Biologically, you are unnecessary to the nursing task. Psychologically, you are very important. Whenever possible, you should be with your wife as she nurses. Praise and adore your wife as she fulfills her maternal role.

Sometime in the early months of nursing, there will be times in the middle of the night when your wife will wish that she was not nursing. She will visualize you getting up in your bare feet, walking half asleep across the cold floor to the baby's nursery, picking up the crying infant, trying to comfort it while the bottle warms, then burping and changing it after feeding while she sleeps contentedly through it all.

You can pick up your crying infant, bring it to its

half-asleep mother, hold the two of them together in your arms, and gently sing to them. Burping is something anyone can do, as is diaper changing. Thus, you can share the nocturnal task, spelling your weary wife.

Nursing time provides a richly appropriate time for family devotions. The Word of God is spoken, and the people of God pray to Him while their infant quietly feeds. I wish that someone would prepare a devotional booklet with two parts: meditations for nursing mothers as they nurse and family devotions for husbands and wives as she nurses.

If you already have children, don't exclude them from feeding times, even if your wife nurses. Those are golden moments when she can hold her nursing infant in one arm and her next youngest child close with the other. Older siblings can gently touch or pat their little brother or sister. Later on, when your wife quits nursing, all family members can take their turn, as they are able, to give the child its bottle.

If your infant is bottle fed, you and your wife need to make sure it is not ignored during feeding. This problem doesn't usually occur during nursing because the mother must hold her child close. A bottle can, however, be propped upon a baby's chest and the infant ignored. Or the baby can be held in one arm with a bottle in its mouth while the parent reads a book held in the other arm. Don't let feeding your infant become as impersonal as when you and your wife sit at breakfast, each absorbed in a different section of the morning paper, indifferent to one another.

Your Infant's Developing Personality

Your small child is a person, a very unique person, and it needs to be treated as a person. Note its individual characteristics and mannerisms. Enjoy them. Parents miss out on most of the joys and blessings of parenthood if they do not cherish every moment they can spend with their children, just being with them. Enjoy their behavior. Observe their unique personalities as they emerge and develop.

Making It through the Night

Your infant's early days will also have their negative side for you and your wife. Sleeping infants are very noisy. They sleep with total physical involvement. They shift around, snuffle, grunt, and groan. Their nasal passages are initially swollen and often filled with mucus. You wake up and want to blow your child's nose. You wish it could be more quiet. Then your child is suddenly totally quiet—not a sound, not even breathing.

Desperately you arise to perform the Heimlich maneuver or CPR or whatever one does to a child who has stopped breathing. Then, with a loud snort, your little infant starts breathing noisily again. Gratefully you return to bed only to have the same experience a few hours later.

There is no alternative. Your child has to sleep out of earshot of its father. Don't worry! Your heavenly Father has equipped mothers with an infant radar detector that works incredibly well. They can hear their infant hiccup from the opposite end of the house. Frustratingly, they can do that and at the same time hear absolutely nothing you may whisper right next to them in bed. This experience is often the first postnatal indication that your personal relationship with your wife is going to be different.

Reestablishing Intimacy with Your Wife

From a physical standpoint, intimacy with your wife has been different for some time. In the latter months of her pregnancy, she was physically less and less accessible. Other than kissing at arms length, she was unable to satisfy your sexual needs. She was completely happy, fully immersed in her changing body and its anticipated fruit. Her body had few other interests.

You, on the other hand, had no such diversion. In the pious hope that a few months of unwilling celibacy would be worth the expected child, you have contained yourself and suppressed all the feelings of frustration that inevitably arise.

After the euphoria of birth, your life together gradually settles into a comfortable pattern. Thoughts of resuming your former sex life come to mind—your mind, not hers. She seems completely satisfied with matters as they are. In self-defense you look up all those passages in the Epistles that tell us that the wife's body belongs to her husband and the husband's to his wife—a viewpoint that in the early months and years of your marriage your wife embraced as eagerly as you.

Now she points out that obviously the Epistle writers were ignorant or indifferent to the fact that a nursing mother's body belongs first and foremost to her infant, and, for a time, that's all one woman's body can handle! How humiliating for the male ego! Your offspring is your rival for your wife's affection and her body.

As the situation does not improve, you find yourself hating that greedy little monster as it dominates your wife's time. You feel incredible moments of hatred, petty thoughts of annoyance, childish jealousies that you have not felt since elementary school. Those are the moments to realize that the battle has begun, not between you and your offspring, but between you and the devil. Yes, in this most blessed time of fatherhood, the devil tries to drive a wedge between you and your child and a division between you and your wife. It is time for fervent prayer and spiritual care to protect yourself from the temptations that can begin to destroy your marriage.

Eventually your wife makes herself available to you. She needs to be loved tentatively and tenderly, for her most sensitive parts are healing, even after a month. In addition there are new obstacles. Her breasts are enlarged; you hug her closely and she leaks into her nursing bra. Sometimes her fiercely sucking infant makes her nipples so sensitive and tender that your slightest touch and embrace are agony for her. The two of you, with a spirit of mutual understanding, will work out a satisfactory physical relationship in the postnatal days.

The First Bath

My wife and I developed the custom that I gave each child its first bath. It probably began because, as we approached our firstborn's first bath, my wife, who had been confident about other matters, was pathologically fearful that our soaked and soaped infant would slip from her hands into the tub. Irrational though the fear was, she insisted that I do the first bath and she stand ready, warm bath towel in hand, to receive the freshly washed infant. So it continued with each subsequent infant's first bath.

First baths can be traumatic both for infant and parent. In the womb, your infant is held closely by its mother's expanding uterus. After birth that confinement is gone, replaced usually by a closely wrapped blanket and the loving confinement of parental arms. At bath time all such constraints disappear. Garments are removed. Your infant's body notes the change of temperature. The child is lowered into an unconfining environment, the tub. In addition, if it is rapidly lowered into the warm bath, your child will experience vertigo and another tactile change, the feel and temperature of the water. Your infant is petrified with fear! It cannot handle this barrage of sensations, and it screams uncontrollably.

Instead, slowly and carefully undress your child, talk or sing to it soothingly, hold its little limbs closely. Cover your child with a cloth diaper and gently lower it into the water, the wet diaper closely covering and protecting it from cooling air currents. Wash your infant gently, a little at a time, beginning with the feet. Infants don't like water running over their heads and down their face, so use great care above the neck. Expect to get wet in the process! The wet diaper can be gently whisked off in the tub before transferring the infant to your wife's arms, where she holds a large, warm, soft, turkish towel.

3
LIVING WATER

In the Middle Ages, infants in physical distress were baptized immediately after birth, as they usually are today; those who were not in danger of immediate death were usually baptized the following day. Today it has become customary to baptize when the mother is sufficiently recovered from her delivery to attend formal worship and when godparents can be present. The Baptism of your infant shouldn't be unnecessarily delayed. Through Baptism certain changes take place relative to and within your child that are essential for its spiritual development.

It is hard for you to imagine it as anything other than pure and sinless as your child lies peacefully within your arms. But through no fault of its own, as a descendant of our first parents, it is not sinless. Your child is born alienated and apart from God. It is your child, but it is not a child of God. By Baptism God becomes your infant's adoptive Father; your child becomes His child.

Your child doesn't do anything to become a child of God. It doesn't look different or act differently after its Baptism. Nothing shows to indicate that a change has taken place, but it has.

Called by Name

From a very practical standpoint, from the moment your child has been baptized, God the Father knows it by name and loves it with all His being. He does not think of your child as just a tiny portion of His creation needing His constant preservation, but as His personal child, like His own only-begotten Son. In a sense, it is somewhat like how you begin to feel about your child when it is born, as opposed to how you feel about all the other babies briefly sharing the hospital's nursery. They are all babies; but that one over there is *your* baby. It is the only one you recognize. Your heart reaches out to it; not to the others. You know it by name.

In the Middle Ages, an infant officially received its name when it was baptized. That was its name day. There being no hall of records or other governmental agency that noted births, weddings, and deaths, an infant's name in the parish baptismal records verified its legal existence. There is, however, more to a name than legal identity. Our names give us a personal identity. We are no longer anonymous. They shape us in the minds of those who use our name.

Some years ago, my wife blessed me with twin daugh-

ters, the last of our flock. Having been warned in advance to expect a multiple birth, we spent the final months of the pregnancy selecting pairs of names that, though different, in some respect were alike, two boy names, a boy and a girl, and two girl names. The two girl names we eventually settled upon were Margaret and Gretchen, the diminutive of Margaret.

The day after the twins were born, my wife called me at home to tell me that someone had stopped by her room to check on the accuracy of the birth information and to record the intended names of the twins. She decided that the twin born first was to be named Margaret and the twin born four minutes later was to be named Gretchen. I reminded my wife that the second twin was both longer and heavier than the first. How could she be "Little Margaret"? I suggested contacting the record office to reverse the names. With complete confidence and great finality, my wife responded, "I can't do that. She is already Gretchen for me, and I have been calling her that all day." So she remained Gretchen and still is, and my wife was right.

God knows your baptized child by name, loves it as an individual, takes a personal interest in its welfare, responds to its needs, and is as close to it as His nearest angel.

The apostles Paul and Peter use the adoption image (Ephesians 1; 1 Peter 1). They also talk of inheritance. Because your child becomes God's child, it is His heir, just as it is your heir by its physical birth. Your child will receive its inheritance from you when you die. You won't be around to watch it enjoy the inheritance. Your child, which already is beginning to enjoy a taste of its spiritual inheritance, will receive its full inheritance from God when it dies and goes to enjoy life with Him and you in eternity.

In Baptism, not only does God change in His attitude toward your child and His relationship to it, He also changes your child in its awareness of and attitude toward Him. God is not part of an unbaptized infant's personal reality. It has no feelings toward God, no awareness of God. In short, your child possesses nothing that would either motivate it or on which it, of its own motivation, could build a relationship with God.

While the spiritual life of a child relates to, and is affected by, its physical, emotional, and intellectual development, that is not its source. Baptize your infant as soon as possible after birth. Baptism generates a spiritual life within your infant and begins its development. Baptism is more than the ceremonial application of water to an infant accompanied by the invocation of the Holy Trinity, Father, Son, and Holy Spirit. Our Lord and St. Paul describe what happens as being "born again" (John 3, Romans 6). The infant acquires a new self, in addition to the self with which it was born. Paul refers to them as the "New Man" and the "Old Man" respectively (Eph. 4:22–24).

God has called your child by name and claimed it as His. Your baptized infant is already aware of its divine Father. The Holy Spirit will work through you and your child's godparents to keep your child close to Him.

Family Worship with Your Child

From the very beginning, include your child in the worship and spiritual activities of your family and the larger family, your parish. An infant can participate in the private devotions of its family even though it cannot speak. Help your infant fold its hands during the early months of its life when it has little control over its movements.

For your child to develop spiritually, it must necessarily be treated as one who knows and loves God, included as a participant in your family's worship. Though it does not speak your language, the Word of God should be read and proclaimed in its presence. Others may pray for it in its presence, as well as on its behalf. Formal prayers, such as the Lord's Prayer, can begin to become a part of your young child's liturgical vocabulary. Your wife, while nursing, may use the occasion to share with your child what St. Paul called the "pure milk of the Word." She may talk with it about its heavenly Father and pray. As the infant is placed in its crib, a prayer, spontaneous or set, spoken or sung, can accompany it into slumber. If the same prayer is used regularly, your child will accept it as part of its normal routine and, surprisingly early, begin to mouth it as you speak.

Your child's spiritual life needs care, guidance, and a rich spiritual environment for healthy growth. Like a growing plant, your child needs the right soil, water, and growing conditions to mature and prosper spiritually. God's Holy Spirit will help you create the environment within which it grows.

Your little one, whom already you love with all your heart, rests quietly in the protection of God. Although your child's faith is now largely passive, soon, with growing competence and energy, in its own childish way it will begin to respond to the constant flow of affection from God.

Nurturing Your Child's Awareness of God

A child's developmental needs can be best and most easily satisfied in a home headed by its own loving, wedded, natural parents. As the originator of such a family, you are responsible that your child, during its maturing years, successfully achieves what it needs with respect to several very important matters.

Acceptance

A child of God needs to feel wanted—by its parents and by God. Erik Erikson identified the trust/insecurity hurdle as the first a child must successfully surmount if it is to undertake the rest of its life in a healthy psychological condition. The foundation that underlies faith is trust, a confident hope about oneself, one's associations, and one's future. Baptism generates faith. As infants become children of God, they relax, confident of His love.

Your infant can lose that security if it does not also experience family acceptance. As your child grows older, it transfers the personal feelings it gets from parental treatment to God. If it becomes accustomed to parental acceptance, it will also continue to feel accepted by God. If your child is unsure of parental acceptance, it may feel that God does not care. If your child's spiritual life has been troubled by human rejection as an infant, as an adult it may well attribute personal misfortune to divine retribution for real or imagined sins.

Acceptance is sometimes identified by a more familiar word—bonding. Your infant needs to attach itself to you and your wife to achieve healthy growth. I have a friend in Great Britain who is a veteran midwife. As soon as a newborn begins to breathe normally, she puts the infant into the mother's arms, encouraging the infant to nurse. Before she cleans the infant, before the umbilical cord is severed, she helps the infant reestablish externally its former internal relationship to its mother. The physical cord is replaced by a psychological bond that will last the rest of its life.

An infant also bonds to a loving father. You cannot give nourishment, but you can hold your child, love it, and share its care with its mother. As you and your wife express your affection for one another in your infant's presence, it develops one bond to the two of you.

Abandoned infants and infants awaiting adoption in a hospital tend to be lethargic, lacking explicit emotional attachment in the external world. In order to thrive, your infant needs love, expressed through close holding, singing, rocking, and other physical signs of affection, in addition to adequate nourishment and physical care.

Children need frequent reinforcement of parental acceptance. When my twins were small, they developed the habit of coming to me or my wife every 15 minutes or so and climbing up on our laps to accept a hug. They didn't disrupt our conversation with visitors or our work. They came briefly, without a word, then left. As they grew older, the span of time between "visits" lengthened. Even as independent collegians, they kept in touch with home through regular telephone calls, often for no apparent reason. Most children have these same needs, satisfying them in various ways, though perhaps not so conspicuously.

Whenever punishment for some misdeed has been administered, reinforce parental acceptance. Punishment, no matter how mild it might be—a frown or a stern word—separates your child from you psychologically. You have indicated that a particular behavior is unacceptable, and you've rejected it. Your child, unable to distinguish itself from its behavior, feels rejected. Hug your child after such a rupture and reestablish your relationship of trust.

Identity

A child usually begins to acquire its identity when it receives its name. An infant's name locates it within the family. If you and your wife have special reasons for the names you've given, share these reasons with your children. It helps their names take on special meaning and value. Often a child is named after a favored relative or friend, thereby creating a bond across generations or family boundaries. Sometimes a child is given a biblical name or a spiritual name, intended to be meaningful to the child throughout life.

Identification with a special place has a powerful effect. Recently my wife and I moved from the home where we had lived for 30 years to a new home two thousand miles to the northwest. Each of our children experienced a sense of loss of the family home, finding different ways of preserving it for themselves before we left. They all cried. We didn't. Not because we didn't care, but because my psychological home was 35 miles northwest and my wife's was 20 miles northeast of the family home.

A few years ago, I was invited to attend an anniversary service at the parish where, many years ago, I had spent a two-year vicarage. I took my wife to see the town that had helped shape my ministry. I was shocked to discover that the parsonage where I had lived had been replaced by the parish school. Little in the church looked familiar. I remembered that the door in the left front wall of the church opened to the corridor and steps that led to my office, the gymnasium, and the stage where my youth activities had taken place. The door would not open. A helpful usher volunteered the information that there was nothing beyond the door. It had all been torn down many years before for a parking lot. Two important years of my past didn't exist anymore!

We shape our children's identity by the past we leave for them to remember, to which they can return in memory even after the bricks and mortar are gone.

A child develops within a series of concentric geographic circles, each larger than the last and varying in importance. Home, community, state, nation—each subtly influences a child's growing awareness of self. During the formative years the closer circles have the greater significance; later, one or more of the larger circles may increase in influence.

Children don't just need to be "from" somewhere; they need to be "of" some family or culture. The question "Mama, where did I come from?" often requires a lesson in history, not biology. Grandparents can play a significant role in establishing their grandchildren's roots. Children love to learn about their grandparents' childhood, what life was like for them, and how they raised their own children. The two generations will form a natural bond. Provide frequent opportunities for your child to talk with its grandparents. I have a friend who tape-recorded conversations with his parents in order that his grandchildren, particularly children not yet born, could have the advantage of great-grandparental insights.

Special occasions of recognition and approval reinforce children's sense of family identity.

When our children were growing up, my place at dinner was at one end of the rectangular harvest table and my wife's at the other, the children sat down the sides. When a child celebrated a birthday, he or she sat at Dad's place for the birthday meal. When my first grandson visited on his birthday, he also sat at that place.

The first time each child brought home a paycheck from a regular job, that child sat at the head of the table. The check was conspicuously exhibited as a sign of family approval and respect for that child as an independent individual and a responsible family member.

My children never succeeded in getting their mother to the head of the table. I suggested that her end was "co-equal," but they didn't accept that as a satisfactory explanation. She did make an exception once when both the children and I insisted. After her first day back at work after many years as a homemaker, we seated her at my place for supper—the chair suitably decorated for the occasion.

Communication

Your infant begins to develop language skills as it interacts with you at home. The process begins as your child nurses. Eye contact, grunts, squeezes, rubbings, and cries all precede verbal communication by many months and create the foundation for it. The more discussion there is with parents and siblings, the more sophisticated conversational skills develop.

Your child will coo first, expressing wordless songs of joy and humming to itself. These words will eventually find their shape as tongues too large to tuck behind baby teeth lisp out initial syllables of communication. Sentences form first in the mind, then in the imagination, before they tumble from uncertain lips.

Mood messages, longings and irritations, and heartfelt desires find significant ways of expression in the home. The language and postures of faith—folded hands, the bended knee, the head bowed low—come most naturally if the home is dedicated to God. Your small child hears you pray and learns to lisp its communication with God from you. Love-talk flowers in the home, verbal kindnesses among kisses and hugs.

A jaw-unhinging yawn signals that your infant has had enough; a quiet half-whimper demonstrates readiness for sleep and signals that even the best of babies can be good just so long.

Writing begins at home, first the difficult letters of the given name and later, when that has been mastered, the family name. Once the talent has been acquired, your child's name soon proudly appears on vacant pages, or in margins of books, or in some hidden place upon a wall. Some children master only their name before schooling begins; others become adept at many words, even unconsciously beginning to read without knowing that they can.

Habituating

For good or for bad, children develop their essential, life-long habits at home. One child specialist claims that all permanent habits are acquired by age 4. You and your wife will influence the habits, virtues, and vices your children will carry through life.

Your children will also mirror your idiosyncratic habits—the physical habits, speech patterns, and mannerisms that mark you. You may want to examine your habits if you do not want to be embarrassed by their replication in your young children.

Children pick up habits everywhere, from sources that are not easy to control. They bring home behavior and language from other children they play with or from adults they admire. Some habits, if temporary, may be amusing. I remember as a small child walking with my legs wide apart, swaying from side to side, to the consternation of my parents who feared that I had begun to develop a hip problem. In fact, I was walking like a telephone lineman who wore spikes affixed to the inside of each lower leg to help climb telephone poles. Many small boys of the time walked in similar manner, like cowboys, bowlegged from years in the saddle. None of us, I suspect, took such habits into adulthood. Many other habits of less indifference we do take with us, and to a great extent they reflect our upbringing.

As a new father, concerned about encouraging healthy patterns of life, examine your own life to identify those undesirable patterns of speech and behavior that, unknowingly, you may pass on to your children. No amount of verbal admonition permanently counteracts a bad example. You cannot expect your children to love and serve our Lord Jesus Christ if you give no evidence of such devotion in your own life.

If a family is composed of active children of God, the members will, in the normal course of life, acquire the habits that will serve them in good stead throughout life. As your children develop language skills, begin to teach simple prayers. Perhaps at first teach them the simple syllables "Amen" or "Abba." Later they can learn short formal table prayers and a bedtime prayer. As they participate in family devotions, your children learn to contribute their own spontaneous prayers and begin to pray without bidding when they are alone.

You, as the father, have the primary responsibility to nourish the relationship begun by the Spirit at your child's Baptism. Associate God with what happens in your family. Call upon Him in prayer. Talk about Him. Sing about or to Him. In all sorts of ways, keep Him present in your family's daily experiences.

Protection

Families—be they birds, animals, or humans—naturally protect their young. Family communities support the weak and helpless until they are capable of fending for themselves. You as a father will tend to have more difficulty adjusting to this parental role than your wife. This is partly because she is usually the source of nutrition for your infant. She has a biological need to protect her little one, like any mother in nature.

Your child needs a place that others enter only with its permission. This need begins very early as part of a larger environment that one might call "the familiar," a living area that your small child knows—its own bed, its blanket, its toys, its room. As your child gives up these initial possessions, it moves to other environments, needing, however, always some thing or some place private to which it can return for security.

God has made you your child's primary protector. When you lose your temper and strike out, you fail as a father. You have destroyed your child's sanctuary. Your home, however, is more than a sanctuary from physical harm. It is the place to which your child can retreat from outside harm, a safe haven where hostile persons cannot enter. Home is a psychological place of respite from the outside world, a familiar place, a place where one can be oneself.

At home, your child always has an advantage over other people who don't belong there. Others are always guests who have to be mannerly and nice whether they want to or not. Family members don't. Your child can go home to regain its perspective when the world outside gets too complicated and bewildering. Bullies are not allowed. Home is a place where your child is always welcomed back.

Thus, from the very beginning, you have to make your home a very special place for your child because it will be more important to it than any other dwelling it will ever have, including the home it creates later. Throughout your child's life, home will remain the place of security, refuge, and privacy even after it is inhabited by strangers or has ceased physically to exist.

Nurturing a Socialized Child of God

An infant soon discovers that because it is part of a family, its freedom of action is limited by the demands and needs of others. It discovers what may popularly be called morality, and it has its first moral experiences within its family. As it hears "No!" for the first time and responds, it begins the lifelong process of trying to make practical sense out of two ideas: right and wrong. In this chapter, we will look at the qualities you can nurture in your child to help it relate to others as God's children.

Moral Sensitivity

Social ethics replace egocentric demands. Single children and young children tend to sustain their egocentric behavior to a later age than children with younger siblings to whom they have to defer. We solved that problem by having twins at the end, a solution open to very few people, and by caring for foster infants.

"Right" and "wrong" are complicated ideas. Legal experts and ethical philosophers dispute their meanings. For little children, however, "right" has a simple, straightforward definition—what I strongly want or what my parents firmly demand.

Your child's problems adjusting to the will of others and suppressing its own demands tend to ease after about three years of life. Your little independent, confrontational ego suddenly becomes "mother's helper," rejoicing in its ability to assist others. Helping your child perform simple helpful tasks introduces it to the larger world of conventional morality.

Obeying

Born in sin, we do not naturally obey others, yet we need to learn to obey if we are to survive to adulthood. We are led astray by our ignorance and our sinful urges. Most children, as they move toward their third year, begin to act willfully. Having developed walking and running skills and some digital dexterity, they can be dangerous to themselves. Although it often begins during the third year and seldom ends much before the fourth, we call this time, "the terrible twos."

You will need patience and ingenuity to survive this time. Your small child is not a living expert; it tries its best. Your child wants to dress itself. It wants to make decisions. You will need patience with your little one's shortcomings and ingenuity to escape its efforts to defy you. As soon as you face a personal confrontation with your child, your child has won the competition of wills it created.

Your task will be more difficult because of your child's limited language skills, though it understands more than it lets on. You cannot calmly reason with your young child. You cannot turn your child's developmental clock back to the time before its ego emerged, when it obeyed every command. Verbally and physically abusive parents seem to command perfect obedience. However, they produce a child who is docile, lacking in personal initiative, or one whose submissiveness masks an unwilling obedience, a smoldering hostility that may grow over the years to explode suddenly in violent or bizarre behavior.

You have a more difficult task—to help your child deliberately obey, controlling its impulses and desires. God calls us to help our children grow up to be autonomous adults, self-reliant, confident, and capable to make their way independently through life, yet always submissive to His will. This process begins when your child learns the meaning of the signal "No!" and pauses a moment before touching something it suspects may be a "No!" object, waiting for parental approval before continuing.

As you help your child become obedient, first, be consistent. Don't use the "No!" signal without enforcing it or it will lose its usefulness. Second, don't use it excessively. Try to change the situation so that you can praise as well as forbid. Third, while disobedience to the "No!" signal must result in a consequence your child does not like, obedience to the "No!" signal must be accompanied by praise—Good boy! Good girl!—to have a more powerful and lasting effect. Finally, keep a sense of humor. A confrontation that is converted into a situation where both father and child can laugh at themselves is already diffused.

Don't take early confrontations too seriously or, when the first occurs, suspect that the Baptism didn't take and you have a child of the devil on your hands. You have a child of God who loves you deeply but wants a bit more independence than you have granted.

Disobedient children act from ignorance or wrong motivation. We need to distinguish between the two lest our response be inappropriate. If the action is done from ignorance, your child needs education; if from wrong motivation, it needs correction. As your child learns to obey, it needs admonition when it does wrong and encouragement to do better.

As a child in a home that serves our Lord, your little one should begin to wait its turn, learn that crying will not work as a device to get its way, discover that accidents can happen even when it is careful, and find out that everyone has rights that need to be respected. Each of us at some time or other has to perform disagreeable tasks when we would rather not. Perhaps one of the hardest things for your child to accept is that not everything it wants is good for it and some things it believes are unpleasant may very well be good. I suspect, however, that no child ever believes that its older siblings should have privileges that it is not allowed.

Sharing

While most small children seem almost spontaneously to learn "Mine!" as they clutch a toy to themselves, they do not naturally share these possessions with others. During their formative months, they regularly receive from others and are not called upon to give or to share. They do not know how to share.

Your child will have to develop the habit of sharing as it becomes sociable and enjoys interchanges with its parents. Begin forming the habit in late infancy when your child can hand an object to someone else and receive it back. Ask your child for the object it is holding. Return the object and laugh with your child. After a while, pause longer and longer before returning the object. Your child has now learned giving—a part, but not all of sharing.

When small children begin to share, they assume that what they have given will be returned. Your little one will share its cookie with someone else. Expecting to get it back intact, your child is horrified to discover that a large chunk of the cookie has disappeared. It begins to cry. To ease the trauma of learning how to share, your child needs some sort of recompense for loss. Perhaps at first your little one can get something it likes in return for what it gave. At a minimum, your child needs recognition and praise until it has grown accustomed to sharing without expectation of return.

You must be careful, however, not to give the impression that one gets something good in return for sharing. Many adults think if they do good things for God they can get what they want from Him—the essence of pagan theology.

Your child will reach the next stage of learning to share when it does something spontaneously for someone it loves and is surprised by their expression of appreciation. Your child may begin to give away things to all persons for whom it cares in order to receive their warm thanks in return. Transition from sharing with members of the family to persons who are not family occurs next, usually with playmates, often involving toys or food.

Generous children are easily taken advantage of by others who do not reciprocate, whether it be in the home or in other company. Often the sharing child is temporarily popular because it can always be counted on to give without complaint. If you are blessed with such a child, help it to understand that sharing has limits and to recognize that people's spiritual life is not helped if they are accustomed to and expect to always receive.

As your toddler grasps the idea of sharing physical items, encourage it to share opinions and thoughts with you. From an early age your child needs opportunities to express opinions on family decision making. A child regularly skipped over or never heard loses its motivation to share and does not feel a part of its most intimate community, its own family. As your child begins to enjoy sharing, it will spontaneously express its ideas and suggestions as a full-fledged, active member of the family. Obviously such expressions need limitation to matters upon which your little one is competent to make suggestions: the choice of a family meal, entertainment for the evening, or the color of its room.

You need daily to share time with your child, one on one, treating your little one as an important person, particularly if you are away at work most of the day. Your child, in turn, needs to share with you and your wife the experiences of the day. When your child is older, going on trips or overnights, it needs to be received home with enthusiasm and eagerness to share its experiences. The father is especially treasured who communicates to his child, "I missed you while you were gone." Children do it. When a parent has been gone and returns, they cling to him or her as if afraid the parent will go away and never return.

My daughters loved to make welcome-home signs. They planned welcome-home dinners, making each return a festive occasion. As high school or college students, when they were gone on an extensive school tour in this country or overseas, each of them shopped to bring home a gift for everyone. They copied me who, whenever I traveled on academic business, brought each one something as a souvenir. At first it was simple things such as sugar, salt, or pepper packets from airline meals or a bag of salted peanuts with the airline logo on it. The gift was not important. Being remembered was. Later, of course, small purchased gifts were more appropriate, tailored to individual taste. My daughters insisted that I bring something special for their mother too.

Children unaccustomed to sharing at home often have difficulty sharing when they enter school. If, in addition, their unwillingness to share with their peers is defended by their parents, they will continue to have difficulties sharing as they mature. Given a healthy sharing family, your child will learn to share without difficulty during the school years and continue the practice into adult life.

Contributing

Closely related to the activity of sharing in relationships is the chance to make a contribution to the welfare of a group. In some families, little or no contributing takes place. Husband and wife seek their own personal satisfactions; children are neglected. This type of family often breaks up, each member seeking satisfaction elsewhere, the children drifting off or becoming wards of the state.

Contributing ratios vary from family to family. In some families, the mother does most of the contributing; in others the parents contribute and the children take. In an occasional family, the children slave for tyrannical parents. Most families fall somewhere in between these extremes, parents usually contributing somewhat in excess of what might be expected and children less than what they could contribute. The participation of parents in the normal nature of family responsibility tends to range from total contribution to each infant's welfare, to a gradual decrease over time, to virtually nothing when their children are grown.

You will find as a father that the critical years are those during which your child can increasingly contribute to the family's welfare but will not if it is not asked or allowed. Unless you are aware of the guidance and example you need to provide, your child will grow up as the constant recipient of parental care and will approach matrimony looking for someone who will continue that parental care. Given the chance, on the other hand, your child will be amazingly thoughtful, at times moving you to grateful tears.

Contributing to the welfare of others will not

come naturally to your child. But, as you hold your child and warmly assure it of your love, its love for you will flow out to your family in the form of happy squeals and smiles at the sight of you. About the age of three, toddling about and self-sufficient, your son or daughter will run its little legs off being mother's or father's helper. Be they big or small, those who feel loved want to do loving things in return. A loving family discovers that its mutual affection increases the happiness of every member exponentially.

I suspect that when most families were not as affluent as they are now, such contributions by members of the family were more common. In my own family, my father's siblings all went to work after high school to help pay their oldest brother's tuition to study for the ministry. No one else in the family could go to college. My mother, who was the eldest in her family, began work after one semester of high school because her father's salary was inadequate to pay the expenses of a growing family. You can probably tell similar stories.

Supporting

Contributing to family planning and welfare leads inevitably to mutual support of one another. Every family has its difficult times filled with days of sickness, worry, fear, and guilt. In such times, family members become critical supports and provide assistance for one another.

Developing family support begins at your infant's birth as you and your wife express mutual affection and care for one another. It grows each time that you set an example by looking for ways to help and pleasantly surprise other members of your family. Your small child will sense the warm feeling of being important to its family, and the comfortable feeling of being surrounded by security. In building an atmosphere of love and security for your infant, you are giving your child a small taste of the great love and care God shows us.

Without any prompting from us, my daughters began to establish a telephone network with one another as they left, one by one, for college. Knowing how I worried when they had problems, they often contacted one another—sometimes their mother—to share fears and concerns. They let me in on the problem when everything was all right once again.

Socializing

In *Politics*, Aristotle demonstrated that the family is the first natural community; all others are based upon it. While human beings may very well be familial by nature, we don't seem to enter the world with an innate sense of social accommodation. Family experiences will determine the sort of social graces your child will develop.

Some people naturally seem to be quiet, private persons, while others are noisy and outgoing. Beyond these broad natural bents, family nurture will begin to shape your child. For good or for ill, your small child takes on the values and behaviors of its home. From that small community, your little one ventures forth into others, carrying its values and behaviors with it. Your task as the head of your child's first social community consists in helping your child to be open and competent, to respond successfully to novelties of person and action.

Your child cannot be open to others without being sure of itself. Paul wrote exuberantly, "I can do all things through Christ, who gives me my strength." Little ones, richly loved by God and parents, often shame us with their confidence—when they are not scaring us half to death by their daring!

During the growing years, you will need to help your little one steer a safe course between rash behavior and fear of novelty. Begin praying now that your child may grow as an adventuresome saint of God, ready always for new places and new ways to be God's person in a darkened world. Surround your child with affection and care and the knowledge of God's great love for us expressed in His Son. Your child will venture forth into the world with a sure trust in God, supported by His Holy Spirit.

Nurturing a Cultured Child of God

At birth, your child enters a rich fabric of culture. Your child must learn what it means to be a member of your family, church, community, nation, and world.

Organizing

Culture begins with the awareness and exercise of order. Children begin to organize their lives within the context of the family. They find their place within it, and from that place, begin to think about who and what they might become. Families may themselves be unstructured, verging on chaos; they may exhibit varying degrees of structure, the amount of order varying from time to time. In this context, a growing child learns how to express itself and how successfully to insert what it wants among the demands and wants of other family members.

The needs of your newborn infant will demand priority in your family. After a time, however, its physical needs become less vital, and other matters may become more important. A time will come when feeding can wait until the phone has been answered! Your child can cry for five minutes until you or your wife get dressed and hold and soothe it. Your infant, without planning on your part, will begin to learn delayed gratification and to coordinate its needs and desires with those of others.

As your child grows in this atmosphere of give-and-take, it will begin to learn how to wait its turn for using the bathroom, the hair dryer, eventually even the family car. Unconsciously, your infant is beginning to develop the organizational skills it will use through life.

As a wise father, you should intentionally provide appropriate opportunities for each child to plan and organize some event. One such event might be the celebration of your child's birthday. If your child plays an active role in organizing and working on the various arrangements, not only will it find the party more enjoyable, it will begin to learn how to plan. Helping prepare a meal, setting a table, arranging a clothing drawer or a toy shelf, planning a menu, organizing a day's schedule—all provide opportunities to learn organizational skills.

Although organizing demands the wise allocation of time to tasks, don't expect your young child to have a sophisticated understanding of time. One of our little neighbors conceives of the future as "next week." Her birthday, the time when she is going to clean her room, the next day—all lie in that ambiguity called "next week."

A child may be excessively conscious of time. We once promised one of our daughters that she could go to camp the following summer. Two days later she reported that she had no clean clothes. She had neatly and carefully packed all her clothing and other needed possessions into her backpack. She was ready for the anticipated trip that, unfortunately, lay three months in the future. It took my wife a week to persuade her to unpack.

An activity related to planning is "budgeting for," which involves the activity—often frustrating to a child—of "saving up for" something. "Budgeting for" teaches many valuable lessons, foremost of which, I think, is an appreciation of how much things cost, either in terms of labor or money. A child who has worked for a possession tends to take better care of it than if that object was acquired with little or no effort. To some extent, care for the possessions of others tends to increase when children learn how much effort is necessary to produce an object.

I feel sorry for children who have the misfortune to come from well-to-do homes with indulgent parents. Such children do not tend to acquire a very useful set of values relative to material possessions, or respect for others' possessions. Most urban vandalism, I suspect, is done by two groups: young people who possess nothing and are unlikely to acquire anything of their own soon and, particularly in suburbs, wealthy young people who have never had to work for anything in their lives and who do not respect the property of others.

Teach your child the joy of "working for" something. He or she may sometimes learn, after having worked for a particular goal, that it was not worth the effort. Your child may also learn that when it is working and saving for some goal, it may have to give up something else. Taking a morning paper route sacrifices sleep, late-night television, and early-morning school activities. If your child gets a Saturday job, it will not participate in certain school sports. Your child will learn the value of trading off one set of values for another. As the saying goes, "There is no free lunch." Teach your child to ask, "What sacrifice must I make to get what I want? Do I want to pay that price?"

While waiting for something, your child will discover the pleasure of extended anticipation, a dimension of the emotional life that is never experienced in the world of instant gratification. Many years ago, because of a slower transportation infrastructure, we all had to wait for our material desires to be satisfied. Mail-order companies played the role of the super stores of today. Many of us grew up eagerly awaiting the arrival of the Christmas toy catalog every October. We leafed through it and went to sleep dreaming of toys we hoped we were going to get. Some of our best memories are associated, ironically, with the delicious anticipation of toys we never got—my electric train, for instance.

Informing

Orienting your young child to the world and assisting it to acquire the skills necessary to survive begins with such simple skills as learning how to walk, talk, feed itself, and use the toilet. Animal parents perform similar tasks for their young. The acquisition of personal history and culture sets human development apart. A baby robin grows up in a nest much like any other robin's nest and learns how to be a robin. Human homes differ remarkably from one another, even when they are tract houses, physically similar yet culturally unique.

When a couple establishes a home, the two, husband and wife, create a cultural environment within which they will nourish their young. Some of the activities and artifacts replicate those of their respective parental homes; some are literally parental artifacts, given to help start the home; some are original to that family. You and your wife are no different.

As your child grows, its life will be informed by

the topics of conversation; the quality of music played; the sorts of television programs watched; the family library of books, music, and other electronic devices; and supplemental activities and materials of your own manufacture or doing. You may read stories to your child, tell it made-up stories, and teach it your favorite songs from childhood. Homemade stories have the advantage of originality and relevance, particularly if members of the family are participants in the imagined plot.

As your child gets older, you may encourage it to make up stories. With its friends it may create plays. All such activities stimulate the imagination and help children connect together larger and larger numbers of items into coherent wholes. Storytelling and acting out stories also give your child opportunity to be "center stage" and to experience family approval.

One year, while on sabbatical from university teaching, my family and I lived in the Cascade Mountains at a spiritual retreat center where I was lecturing. Sunday afternoons in the winter were times of complete boredom for the children of that community; nothing to do and nowhere to go in the deep snow. Purely by accident, they began to gather at our home for story time. We thought of a little duck, named Waddle Daddle, who thought he was human. Every Sunday he had a new adventure that we made up together.

Children of God need creative experiences so that when they are adults, they will always be discovering new ways to serve God. Infants are ingenious in discovering how to cope with life in the external world, but they are not—fortunately—particularly creative. Otherwise we would never get any sleep! But their creative powers, in time, need to be developed. The arts are particularly useful in stimulating your child's imagination and creativity.

Beyond their powers to stimulate creative thought, the arts provide a variety of avenues whereby God can be presented to human beings. The medieval church, limited by the illiteracy of most of its people, compensated by the spoken word, songs, pictures, architecture, drama, and dance. The darkness of the age came to an end when the Word of God was printed in the tongue of everyday people and joined the arts to exhibit the majesty and grace of our loving God. Your child deserves no less rich an approach to its Father God, both to reveal Him and to enrich the variety of ways to praise Him.

One of the first arts that can effectively be used is music. Children experience music with their total being. Watch a small child as a band plays. If it is standing, it begins to march about. If seated, its legs begin to swing up and down in rhythm to the music. It bobs its head and claps its hands or sways rhythmically to the music. Overwhelmed by the beat and melody, it may run about, spin, or roll over and over as it responds expressively to what it hears.

Music appreciation, however, can begin for your child even before that when you sing it to sleep or when, wide awake, it lies in your lap. As you sing something rhythmic, move your little one's hands in rhythm to the music. Then shift to the legs, moving them up and down, like walking, in unexpected sequence. Alternate with a gentle nuzzle of your infant's exposed belly or a gentle tickle of the ribs. Your little one will, in interaction with you, begin to enjoy not only the pleasure of fatherly attention but also the joy of rhythmic melody.

When a small child is able to walk, music leads naturally to dancing. Primitive cultures have not lost this link; civilization has largely destroyed it. After a certain age, we begin to frown upon children running around or "showing off." So they lose their creative impulses. Formal education restricts their free movement further, and they walk in lockstep, shamble along, or gracefully glide under an imaginary book rather than exhibit their natural grace in dance.

Assuming you have not lost all of your youthful physical abandon on the dance floor to the gravity of fatherhood, you can lead your small child in any open space at home through self-satisfying hops, skips, and gyrations.

One year my wife made tutus for my three oldest

daughters, ages 4 to 8, as surprise Christmas presents. They were simply lengths of netting attached to a strip of cloth that could be wrapped about the waist and tied. They were designed to be worn over a T-shirt and a pair of tights: instant ballerina. In no time, each of them tied ribbons to a pair of slippers.

They posed; they stood, arms akimbo; they pirouetted. They bowed with graceful waves of their arms. They practiced walking like ducks. They pretended to stand on their toes. In every respect they fancied themselves prima ballerinas. Poor old dad was assigned to the discard pile of irrelevance. He was too tall to practice lifts with them and too clumsy for anything else—besides which, he probably did not have very good-looking legs. Thus we fathers are rendered obsolete by the classics. I got my revenge when I danced with their bridesmaids at their weddings. Each commented on my grace!

Many children enjoy dramatic production. Once again, you begin during infancy, making faces at your child: a solemn wink, a big smile, an exaggerated look of surprise. The use of hand puppets fascinates older infants and toddlers. They are intrigued by the persona of the puppet. When they are a little older, they examine the empty sleeve, puzzled about where the person went. Soon they can begin to do their own shows, perhaps with puppets or just with a face drawn on the side of their closed fist with a non-toxic marking pen.

When your child is ready, the experience of the arts in a professional setting—particularly performances designed for children—can greatly expand its experience. Many communities or colleges with active theater groups present drama for children. Symphonies give children's performances, as do many ballet companies. An important adjunct to the home, the public library with its children's room and story times continues the process of the love for literature that you begin.

Your infant struggles to understand and communicate with our foreign world. You need to point the way to a richer, more satisfying world than that which simply satisfies our elemental needs. You don't need urging to desire a life of material comfort for your small infant. But you also need to provide a cultured and cultivated life for that same child. And, most precious of all, pray that this tiny boy's or girl's relationship with God might be as rich and full and vivid as it ever was for Dad.

Developing Values

Most of a child's values accumulate early in life. You may find it difficult to think of your infant as a worshiping child of God. You may feel that it does not belong with the worshiping community on the Sabbath. You may feel that it would be best to keep your child at home or put it in the church nursery while the older folks worship. By that well-intentioned action, you subtly affect your infant's spiritual development.

At the same time, when your child is older, forcing its unwilling participation or punishing it for being "bad" in church also creates subtle rebellions that surface many years later. I have known many a university graduate student who harbors strong hostility to any sort of organized Christianity because of compulsory attendance at church during childhood. You will walk the difficult path between these extremes of exclusion and compulsion as you shape your child's spiritual life.

God promises you: "If you bring up your child in the way I want for it, when it is old, it will not depart from it." Be careful that your child enjoys the service and worship of its heavenly Father. This is most likely achieved if you, its earthly father, share that joy with it.

Creating Traditions

Deliberately or not, each family creates its own customs. Some preserve grandparent's and parent's traditions, some come from other homes, some are original. Some homes develop a rich varied tradition; others a poor mix. Family traditions are, perhaps, the richest product each member takes from the home, customs forged and preserved together through the growing-up years.

Ethnic roots are one of the richest sources of tradition, with special dress, dances, foods, unique holidays, verbal expressions, and unique customs at religious holidays such as Christmas or Easter.

Some customs are unique to particular families, preserved for hundreds of years. In my family, the oldest son of the oldest son for hundreds of years was always named William Henry Frederick, after the Hohenzollern royal family.

One family's custom required that, after the first child was born, the father began to carve figures from wood for a family creché. Each year he was to carve another until the family had a complete set. I adopted that custom for my family. Unfortunately, having carved the baby Jesus and His parents, I became too busy to continue. One Christmas when my son was 3, the Christ Child figure disappeared. My wife found it under my son's pillow the next morning. She returned it to the creché only to have it disappear again and reappear in the same hiding place. That son now has a little boy of his own, for whose sake he requested those three figures. I hope he is not too busy to carve some more figures for his little boy.

Traditions hold a family together. Tevye, in *Fiddler on the Roof* was not far wrong when he sang about the need for "tradition." Each culture, and each religious community, has its unique occasions that enrich and give life meaning. Your greatest gifts to your children, apart from the faith you and your wife share as loving Christian parents, are the rich customs that they will always remember and often introduce into their own homes.

Sexuality

Children approaching puberty are frequently unsure about their sexuality. Recent social changes have destroyed many accepted male and female roles and acceptable ways of relating to one another. We live in a society to some extent shaped by people whose aberrant development dominates the media with their confusions.

Your child's sexual self-identification develops unconsciously in your home. Your child becomes what it sees and admires in you and your wife and what it perceives as the sort of person you both desire. Most of this development occurs without conscious awareness, either by parents or children.

Both boys and girls need, at some time or other, to accept their gender. Healthy sexual development begins when you and your wife rejoice in your child, regardless of its gender. Disappointment about gender should yield to thankfulness that your child is healthy and your wife is well. Beyond these feelings comes the joy that here is another potential resident of the kingdom of God to be cherished, loved, and fitted for lifelong service to Christ.

Following birth, mothers have the primary responsibility to foster the joy of maleness in their sons; fathers should encourage the joy of femaleness in their daughters. During the growing-up years, physiological development gives the advantage to girls over boys at first, but later, the advantage reverses.

If you have a son, you may experience the shock of discovering a rival for your wife when your 3-year-old announces that it's just a matter of time before he grows up and marries her. Asked about your status, your son will vaguely dismiss the matter as irrelevant and go off to be with his mother. This event signals that your son approves of you enough to want to be you. And he loves his mother so much that he wishes the relation would last forever. Freud called this the Oedipal stage, a natural and usually harmless time, unless a child is unable to develop beyond it, remaining dependent on its parents.

Girls go through this, too, at the same age. They discover how wonderful it is to be daddy's girl and "innocently" crowd between you and your wife on the sofa. Your wife has to be content to be "the other woman" until the phase is over.

Children think about being a father or mother. Even at a surprisingly young age, they worry about whom they will marry. My son once remarked that getting married was easy for me because Mom was there waiting. He would have to go outside the family to marry some stranger whom no one knew.

During this same stage, your child demonstrates that it is aware of its sexuality and is attempting to come to grips with it. Your child will fantasize about being an adult. It plays "house," sometimes even engaging in role reversal. Your child and its playmates will take turns being the father, mother, or child. But it's unlikely your youngster will feel any of the urges of puberty. It may try kissing someone but will probably find it unsatisfying.

Some children are satisfied simply to be near a favored parent or to be a "gofer" for him or her. Some experience hostility toward the parent of the same sex. Others can be jealous of the attention the parents bestow on one another. It varies from child to child.

You will need to be careful how you treat your children at this time. Don't misinterpret their advances or treat them coldly. Most children move from this "daddy's girl/mamma's boy" stage into one where, for all practical purposes, they are sexually neutral. A year or so later, they become gender isolates, girls associating with girls and boys with boys—even within the family.

Children, for the most part, seem to take this sexual merry-go-round in stride. They emerge into the age of puberty, their hormones pumping furiously to stimulate them to a new appreciation for the opposite gender outside the home and their parents within it.

No amount of careful instruction about sexual matters exceeds the effect of the example you and your wife give your children, not only in how you treat them but in how you treat one another. Parents who battle one another, compete with one another for dominance, or batter one another teach more by action than by words. On the other hand, parents who express affection for one another, defer to one another, and care for one another reinforce the message they have taught their children about how to be a man or a woman of God and how to make a marriage.

Caring

Caring differs from *caring for*. Anyone with a kind heart can *take care* of someone. Only those who love one another care what happens to them. Families are primary caring communities, but, unfortunately, many of them are fragmented by divorce. Some, though intact, don't care, or one or more members of the family feel that no one cares. Children need someone who cares. When no one in the family cares for it, a child may form an attachment to a baby-sitter, a neighbor, a teacher, the family pastor—anyone who seems to notice it and give it personal attention.

Your child equates caring with parents who have time for it and its needs. Ironically, if you often work overtime to provide your child with things you *think* your child wants, your child might think you don't care because you're never "there" when needed.

From the start, you need to let your child know that you care. Make sure your child knows its eternal welfare is more important to you and your wife than anything else. Hug your child regularly and assure it of your continuing love. When it has done wrong, or thinks it has done wrong, your child needs both your forgiveness and the reassurance of your deep affection.

Time spent in simple pastimes with your child means more than expensive gifts. I find it interesting that families noted for the number of orphans and handicapped children they take into their families are often of lower-middle income. They simply love children and, in their humble surroundings with their modest means, give them all the needed nutrients for a rich life.

No new social institution will develop that can successfully replace the family in caring for children. As you begin raising your family, you have an opportunity to help change the pattern of family decline and disintegration. Your responsibility extends not only to God who gave you your child, your wife who carried it, and the child, but also to parents your own age, who need examples of responsible parents.

"Saint" Father

Many of the topics we discussed in the previous chapters could be addressed to any father and mother, Christian or not. This chapter is different. It addresses your role as a child of God, the head of a home composed of children of God.

In a very remarkable way, when your child looks at you, it sees, not only its father, it sees God. As if that were not a big enough burden to bear, your son, at the least, looks to you as a role model to copy when he grows up. I have given this chapter its peculiar title because, for your small child, you have a halo and because, one suspects, that only a saint could succeed at being a father.

The institutional church has sanctified a great number of people through the centuries. St. Paul assures us that we are all saints through Christ's redemptive sacrifice, yet I search in vain among these "official" saints for Saint Father. The vast majority of them were unmarried or achieved sainthood apart from family responsibilities. I wonder how saintly they would have been if they had had to raise a family and care for a wife for a lifetime. Therefore, I salute the anonymous fathers through the centuries who deserved official sainthood but will get their proper recognition only on Judgment Day.

Who Is God?

As your child begins to accumulate names and concepts, one of them is the name "God," obviously the name of a very important person. God is someone who, though unseen, your baptized child loves with its full heart. No one sees God. So it seeks unconsciously to give content to that name by looking for someone who is like God: important, loved by it, male. Only one person fits that description—Dad! Your child will observe your behavior to understand what sort of person God is. Every move you make is a theological move, for it says something about God, correctly or incorrectly, to your child. That is frightening!

You have no way of knowing, until long after, what spiritual effect you have had on your child. Your very behavior shapes your small child's image of God. If you frighten your child, it will be afraid of God; if you are warm and loving, it will feel loved by God. If you are cold and distant, if you are always irritable, if you are gone for long periods of time on business and indifferent when you return, if you are a pushover and can be manipulated, that will contribute to your child's image of God.

How you respond to the sins of your child and its siblings also has an effect. If you do not punish, if you punish severely or punish the wrong one, if you seem weak under pressure, your divine attributes will suffer and your halo tarnish.

Children also assign some divine attributes to their loving fathers. This is why they quarrel and compete with one another at a certain age about the relative capacities of their fathers. Each sees his or her father as omniscient and omnipotent. Your child will also assign to God some aspects of your relationship with your wife. If you are kind, caring, and respectful, your child will see God in that same light.

Not without cause, Paul requires fathers to rule their households and bishops to have their own households in order. Those relationships speak to sensitive children about God more effectively than words.

Father as Role Model

Fathers are role models. You have no choice in the matter. Your child *will* copy you. It may follow you in your career if you seem happy in it. Your youngster may copy your speech, your mannerisms, your choice of language, your manner of walk, your habit of slouching on the sofa, or the way you sit bolt upright with perfect posture.

If you are devout, your child probably will be. If you worship regularly, it will also. If you are super involved in church matters, your child may resent the time you take from it. Church orphans are seldom pious. On the other hand, if you are uninvolved, your child will, as soon as it is able, tend also to be uninvolved.

By this time, being a good father must seem to you a superhuman task. In some respects it is. That is why we pray a lot and study the Word of God a great deal, in order not to mess it up any more than we have. Fathering is difficult; men, by their very nature, don't tend to get together to talk things over with other fathers or form advocacy groups for father recognition.

Spiritual Instruction in Your Home

God calls you to be the spiritual leader of your household. You must not only model; you must teach because modeling is not enough. Let me insert an important spiritual point here. While your child tends to form its initial conception of God by drawing on your characteristics, it does not do that with Jesus Christ, the incarnate Son of God. Nor does your child need to. The Word of God presents Christ to us in rich detail.

Children, when questioned about Jesus, do not

describe their father. Given good instruction, they describe someone of Jesus' historic age and dress when He lived among us. Thus, you must both be like and teach the Father but also introduce our Savior, the Son of God. The Holy Spirit is another matter entirely. By His very nature, He is imperceptible. Hence, we are introduced to Him in His first "modern" appearance on Pentecost by the visual appearance of fire and the auditory sensation of a rushing mighty wind. Your task as spiritual leader in your home lies in bringing your child to an awareness of each Person of the Trinity.

Your responsibility begins with your own life, living in such a way that your love of God is apparent. This means that you and your family include God as part of your normal conversation, lovingly and reverently speaking His name. There was a time in the Old Testament church when the name of God was not spoken, out of awe of His majesty. The sacred initials were written, but the name was never uttered lest the speaker be struck down by lightning for blasphemy.

Fortunately for us, God does not wish to be hidden from His people. He wishes to be addressed personally, as "Father."

Such intimacy is generated by the Spirit's guiding, through God's Word and His Sacraments. Pray and read the Word of God in your baby's presence.

Just as it is protected for a time from disease, apparently by its mother's milk, so the water of baptism keeps your child close to its heavenly Father.

As your child begins to understand language and to speak, teach it "God" words such as "Amen" and "Jesus." The more your family speaks the language of God, the sooner these sorts of words will enter your child's vocabulary.

Developing Spiritual Habits

We tend to be creatures of habit. We need spiritual habits also, routines that are not broken: reading the Word of God at a particular time each day, engaging in private prayer, gathering for family devotions, and attending corporate worship as a family. Pray aloud to God as you tuck your child into bed. As your child begins to speak, lead it to form its own prayers and begin to teach it a set prayer such as "Now I lay me ..."

An early prayer form may take the character of "What I like about you, God," or "Look after the following and bless them, God," or it may be a "Thank-You-God" prayer. Your child's prayers may surprise you by their spiritual insight or by what you didn't think it noticed. These prayers will also make you smile. One of my grandsons prays, "Thank You, God, for Mamma and Daddy, for Grandma and Grandpa, and for 'tucky fried chicken!"

You need to help your child share its thoughts with God frequently, particularly when it is alone. When a problem or a cause for rejoicing arises for you or for the family, pray in the company of your family. This custom of spontaneously turning to God will become second nature for your child. After a time, each child can take a turn in leading the family in its daily prayers.

As you worship regularly with your congregation, your child, held in your arms or later at your side, will begin to "sing" when the congregation sings. Some months thereafter, your child may repeat a line of the liturgy, join in the Lord's Prayer, or recite a phrase of the Creed. When this begins to happen, you help the orientation process by practice sessions at home. Speaking the language of worship at home will help your child participate more fully at church.

Be sure your child's bookshelves contain Bible story picture books and audiocassete tapes. When your child begins to attend Sunday school, use the Sunday school lessons as part of your family's devotional life. You will be amazed what is available from Concordia Publishing House and other religious publishing houses in attractive formats for children.

NOW I LAY ME

Your child has outgrown its crib and is now in its own bed. It can distinguish night from day, familiar faces from strangers. Your infant has been weaned and sleeps through the night. Now begins one of the most delightful times for you in your child's life, the tucking-in time.

Your child is a daytime delight. You play silly little games with it until it is tired. You take turns with your wife feeding it. You contribute to its "cultural growth" by holding it snugly on your lap while together you watch a professional football, basketball, or baseball game on television. You teach it high fives and "Right on!" and all the other gestures and words necessary for a full appreciation of the game as a spectator.

You may have time, now and then, to rock your little child to sleep or to lie down with it after lunch while it begins its afternoon nap. The best time, unless it goes to sleep as soon as it is dark, is bedtime. That is the time your little one conspires with you against its mother to stay awake as long as possible after it has gone to bed.

Let me tell you something about mothers. They

believe bedtime is for sleep. Imagine that! Children don't; fathers don't. Before very long, you will take your little one by the hand about 7:00 or 7:30 in the evening and head off to bed. You will do the bathroom stop, the brushing-teeth stop, the dirty-clothes-in-hamper stop, all those things mothers think are so important. Then, into bed for prayers.

The Bedtime Conspiracy

You may very well have a bit of conversation about God before talking to God. If your little one is tired, it may simply turn over for your goodnight kiss and be off to sleep before you can leave the room. But one night, just as you have tiptoed to the door, a wide awake little voice will summon you back with the word, "Dad?" There's a question. A comment. A request. "Read me a story?" "Can I have a drink of water?" "Dad, what if ... ?" This is the beginning of a conspiracy against the dark—and your wife—that your child will sustain as long as it can, with your delighted help. This is dad/daughter or dad/son time. It's the time when parental barriers and rules are ignored and you just talk heart to heart, honestly and straightforward.

At first this time won't be long, five or 10 minutes out of your evening with your wife, but as time goes by, it will get longer. If your child is organized, there will even be an agenda of items. You talk about this and that. She wants your advice. He has been wondering about that. They want a story.

Your wife calls from downstairs. "Dear, have you fallen asleep?" Her voice is a bit irritated. Your child chuckles conspiratorially; you smile at one another, your finger on your lips for quiet. "In a moment, dear!" you answer sweetly. A few more minutes until you are done talking, then you tuck your little one in with an affectionate hug that is massively returned. Your child buries its head in the covers and turns to watch you leave, its eyes shining with love through the dark.

Nightmares

Sometime, probably in your child's third year, you will be shocked into wakefulness by a scream or the sound of panicked weeping from your child's room. You will discover your offspring, upright in bed, terrified, staring wildly into the night. It will throw its arms feverishly about you and sob out its frightening story. Whatever the content of its childish story, the cause will be the same as any other child's. It has had its first nightmare.

You hold your little one close until it stops trembling; you dry the tears; you make soothing, singing sounds. When your little one has become quiet, you can begin to explain what has happened. Explain that everyone has nightmares now and then, particularly during times of over-excitement or after eating the wrong thing late in the evening. No need to worry. Jesus can drive away such dreams if we ask Him to do it. Your child will soon settle down. It may not even remember the experience the next morning.

Soon after this, your child may begin to be afraid of the dark, resisting going to bed as long as possible, finally even refusing unless accompanied to bed by a parent, the light left on. Children vary in their night fears and the reasons for them, so you will have to experiment as to what works. We usually spent a little more time with our children's bedtime ritual or invited them into our bed for a time, to calm their fears. When they were older, they often crept back to their own bed as silently as they had come, having just checked on the availability of their security place in case they really needed it.

The Child Alarm Clock

One of the most delightful ways of waking up in the morning occurs when a little person crawls onto the bed, sits on your legs, and gleefully crows, "Morning, Daddy!"

I am a night person. My wife is a day person. She always managed to escape this treatment by getting up to make breakfast. I can still hear her sweet voice saying, "Just crawl in with your daddy for a bit until I get the house warmed up and breakfast on." Then came the cold little feet into bed with me.

It's Not Always a Picnic

Even the best-regulated of homes has its times when things go wrong. No matter how saintly your child may be, it is also a sinner—as are you. You need to be aware that your little child will soon reach an age when it will begin to try your patience. Forms of behavior that everyone found cute at an earlier age will become obnoxious. You need to do something about that behavior and about the attitude that underlies it. Neither are good for the spiritual vitality of this child of God whose welfare is your responsibility.

Father as Judge

Several generations ago, the role of judge was assumed to be part of a father's responsibility, as was that of family breadwinner and household head. Many an older adult can remember hearing a frustrated mother call out, "You wait until your father gets home! He'll fix you!"

My generation changed those roles in such a

way that both mother and father assumed responsibility for correcting a child that had begun to develop habits that are not good for it and forgiving it when it had changed. Unfortunately, the generation that has followed us, for a variety of reasons, has left a great many households where no father is present. The result is that the total responsibility for judgment rests upon the mother's shoulders. Hopefully your generation will begin to restore the integrity of families with both father and mother present, both judges and comforters.

As a good father, you cannot avoid the role of judge. You need, however, to avoid two errors: personal bias and judgments that conflict with those of your wife. Personal bias arises easily because your child's behavior that requires you to judge tends to be an act of defiance toward you. Your child consciously and deliberately disobeys you, then waits to see whether it will escape without criticism—a personal thing between you and that little imp! If you allow it to be a personal matter, your child will begin to increase its defiance as it resists you.

Don't Let Sin Grow

Sin is essentially defiance of God, be it by the devil himself or his demonic impulses arising in the heart of a small child. You should not be surprised or dismayed when your own little one begins to display such impulses toward you, its surrogate God-figure in the family. You cannot permit defiance to succeed because it is harmful for your child's spiritual life. Every time it yields to a demonic impulse it weakens resistance to the next temptation.

You cannot deal with defiance on a personal level. Whether you solve the problem by ignoring your little defiant person, diverting it, or changing its mood by making the situation humorous, defiance needs to be drained of its attractiveness for your child. You may be able by sheer force of will, or physical punishment, to intimidate your child; you cannot, however, be satisfied simply to terminate defiant behavior. You may simply force the defiance out of sight and convert it into repressed anger, resentment, or the beginnings of hatred, which may smolder and grow, sometimes for years, until it breaks out in hostile behavior. The motivation of defiance needs to be dissipated and replaced by love, reestablishing that triune relationship shared by the two of you with God. When that relationship is intact, there is no defiance.

Your Child's "First" Sin

Few experiences in life satisfy like the love you have for your small child. Each move, each conscious advance toward intelligent communication, each hug or look of love far surpasses any other human experience. Sinfulness seems impossible in that perfect relationship the three of you have with one another and God.

The first childish defiance of your offspring can be unsettling. Your little one is not very good at defiance. There it stands, sticking out its lower lip, "I WON'T" written all over its tense body. At the same time, it halfway hopes you will interpret this as a joke so it can escape the consequences it already suspects are not going to be pleasant.

You may be shocked. You knew that all human beings are conceived in sin, but unconsciously you believed that maybe your kid was the exception. Now look at it! There it stands, defiant in the fallen forces of humanity, one of the sorry company of sinners of whom you are a leading member.

More likely you will be amused. The little thing looks so cute, another little Napoleon, taking on the world as it knows it. Angry or amused, you must deal with your child's defiance. This is your first indication that it has responded to the wrong motivation within it. Gently you have to help your child restore its spiritual roots.

As you may suspect, the process of reconciliation takes time. It is not solved by a slap, a sharp word, or an order for your child to stand in the corner or go to its room. Nor is it solved if you give it an affectionate hug or ignore its behavior.

In some respects, although one does not want to pursue the analogy too far, your child is showing the first symptoms of spiritual illness. You cannot ignore it any more than you can ignore physical illness. By the same token, don't overreact. Hopefully you do not put your child to bed and saturate the system with juices every time your child sneezes; don't relegate your child to damnation with every offense either.

As your child grows older, its acts of defiance will become more difficult to resolve. To some extent, they are related to its efforts to outgrow the self-centeredness that comes naturally to it from birth. To some extent, these acts of defiance are related to your child's efforts to become independent and self-sufficient. Both of these are necessary if it is to become a fully-developed adult child of God. Your attempts to judge confrontations with your growing child must take these efforts by your child into consideration, lest your responses frustrate them.

God's Word to Fathers

I find it interesting, and probably significant, that the Word of God contains several admonitions for fathers regarding the raising of children and none for mothers. The admonitions are limited in number and length and usually include admonitions for children to obey their parents in the Lord. Yet there they are, jerking us to attention and holding before us the primary responsibility for raising our children:

Fathers, do not exasperate your children; instead, bring them up in the training and instruction of the Lord. (Eph. 6:4)

The "rod" passages from the book of Proverbs (13:24, 22:15, 23:13, and 29:15) have often been terribly abused by fathers and teachers in their interpretation and application. The rod is a shepherd's tool used to gently but firmly direct a wayward sheep toward its proper path. A shepherd would not for a moment think of using the rod to beat a lamb into submission. Why then have so many interpreted such passages to mean they can strike the lambs of God in anger?

Because you are, by virtue of fatherhood, occasionally forced out of your role of approving parent into that of judge and corrector, you need, with love, patience, and the Holy Spirit's guidance, to draw out your child's unique expressions of divine love. Help it overcome those demonic forces from within that would choke off that expression and turn it away from God and from you.

When Your Child Says "I'm Sorry"

God help us to avoid sitting in judgment upon our children! We are called to judge our children, not to sit in judgment upon them. We are not like members of the judiciary but like the members of the medical profession, diagnosing and prescribing for those spiritual illnesses that inhibit our child from being fully the child of God. Our main remedies are confession and forgiveness—confession as a purge and forgiveness as a balm for healing.

A heartfelt confession dislodges shame, and forgiveness washes it away. Children need the therapy of confession, not because we may want it but for their own sake. For a child raised in the love of God, recognizing sins is not difficult; its parents make it aware of them. For a small child, "I sorry" comes easily to the lips. But when your child is a little older and defiance begins to come easy, confession comes with difficulty. You have to find ways your child can relieve the barrier between you that its defiance has created.

You cannot by yourself bridge the gap. Your child must be open to forgiveness. As with hugging, both persons have to have their arms open to one another. You, however, have to create the conditions under which your child will open its arms. Sometimes it needs a little time by itself. Sometimes it needs a reprimand. Sometimes it needs to be deprived of something it values in order to return willingly to its former relationship with you and God. Whatever you do to bring about reconciliation, you must be careful that you do not set off another level of defiance that's stronger than the last. The devil will be attempting to increase the division he has already created.

Many parents fail to be sensitive to this fact, assuming that the action of punishment completes dealing with an act of defiance. It doesn't. Unless you actively seek reconciliation, your child may feel abandoned or harbor a resentment that can become deep-seated. Parents may thus, with the best of intentions for their child's welfare, be unintentionally cruel, lacking sensitivity to their child's feelings.

When I was about 4, I was involved in some sort of disagreement with my mother one cold winter morning. My father, irritated by the noise, angrily suggested that if I didn't like it there, I could find some other place to live. Bull-headed and righteously indignant, I immediately accepted the offer. To my great surprise, my father whipped a small suitcase from the hall closet, threw a few articles of clothing into it, bundled me into my winter coat and hat, and thrust me out into the snow, locking the door behind me.

I still remember standing there, bawling and cold. I also remember being very angry with my father because he had not given me time to get my piggy bank. Before I had a chance to wonder whether I was ready for life on my own, the door was unlocked, and my mother drew me back into the house.

For many years a barrier continued between my father and myself because of what he had done and thoughtlessly left unresolved. I continued to remember that he had not wanted me at home. None of his many subsequent acts of thoughtfulness erased that feeling of abandonment. I finally had to erase it myself as an adult. But, as you can see, I still remember the event and the hurt.

Having opened the way to forgiveness, your child needs speedy forgiveness, accompanied by hugs and other expressions of affection. Then the two of you need time in prayer together to seek the forgiveness of God. Your joint prayer for forgiveness and help to resist the devil's temptation will keep your child aware of its most vital relationship with God.

If confession and forgiveness are done well, you and your child will be closer to one another and to God. Somewhat like the breaking of a bone, the repair, done well, is stronger than the bone was before. After an unsettling experience that we had resolved, I tried to find some way for my child and I to do something together that proved I had now forgotten the unpleasantness. It might be that we went grocery shopping together, or I asked that child to help me with a task, or we served that child's favorite meal. If you follow my example, however, make sure you do it in such a way that your child does not conclude the only way it can get your attention or acquire something it wants is by being "bad."

When You Need to Say "I'm Sorry"

You also sin; don't ever forget it! You will sin against your child. You need to confess your sin and receive forgiveness. Not only will such willing action on your part relieve your conscience and repair your spiritual life, it will enhance you in your child's eyes and ease the way in the future for it to confess a wrongdoing.

Presenting a United Front

Parents disagree with one another about many things. Over a period of time they work out ways of resolving their disagreements. Not surprisingly then, you and your wife sometimes disagree about whether or not your child has done wrong and, more frequently, what ought to be done to correct the situation. If you disagree in the presence of your erring child, you make a fundamental mistake. By disagreeing, you reduce the severity of the infraction. You provide an opportunity for your child to play one of you against the other to get a reduction in penalty or to get off entirely. You and your wife must work together to resolve your child's spiritual conflict.

Many times, one of you will deal with a situation because you are closer to it or more competent to resolve it. In a family with a number of children, one parent can often relate more successfully with a given child than the other. Regardless of how you and your wife resolve potential conflicts with one another, let your child know that you are united in your love and concern for it.

WHEN TO BUY THE BIKE

Someone places a helpless little reddish bundle into your arms saying, "Congratulations, Daddy!" You stand there, feeling more awkward than you ever have in your life, and it squirms. You panic, wondering what will happen if you drop it. Should you loosen the stranglehold you fear you have on its tiny body? Should you clutch it even closer so it doesn't squirm away? Is there a chance that you might squeeze it into the atmosphere like toothpaste from a tube? Your mother resolves the dilemma. "Here, dear, hold it close to your heart."

You won't always have your mother available for advice. But you will have your child until it leaves your home as a grown-up. There will be many conflicts between your protective urges and your child's behavior, particularly as its normal spirit of curiosity and adventure emerges.

You have the advantage of experience over your child. You are accustomed to anticipating multiple possible outcomes and being farsighted. Your infant is not. Its world has one temporal dimension—Now!—and one spacial dimension—Here! That world will soon begin to expand. You will be one of the two primary human guides God has given your child to enable it safely to enter and become comfortable within that world. Inside your home, your wife, whether she is employed or not, will probably be the primary personal guide. Your primary responsibility will consist in making your home as child-safe as you can.

Protecting Your Child

That expression, "child-safe," is ambiguous. At first it will mean making sure that your home is a safe place in which your child can grow up. Later it will mean protecting the physical surroundings you call your home from the destructive actions of your growing child. Both are your responsibilities as father.

Keeping your home a safe place for your child will grow increasingly difficult as it becomes mobile. Almost before you know it, your child will be creeping, then crawling, and then walking, in most cases within the first year of life. One moment, it seems, you are fearing crib death when you don't hear any sounds from the nursery; the next you are praying your child won't self-destruct as it discovers one dangerous thing after another you neglected to put out of reach.

At age 2, your child greets you happily, sitting on the floor with a broad smile on its face. It's holding out an empty bottle of baby aspirin, orange saliva drooling from the corner of its mouth. It has solved the problem of the child-proof cap; you make a quick trip to the hospital emergency ward. The psalmist writes, "He shall give his angels charge over you to keep you in all your ways." You will conclude that those words were intended particularly for children, for one poor, harassed father alone certainly cannot keep his child safe.

Small children blunder into trouble; older children often seem to court it. As their circle of acquaintances grows and playmates increase in number and ingenuity, your child will bring home novel ways of getting into trouble, as well as shocking new vocabulary.

Keeping Up with Your Child

Your child's mobility will also increase. It will progress through a whole series of vehicles. Your infant's earliest days will find it transported in your arms and those of your wife. In short order, you will likely carry it in a sort of bed basket, swaying gently back and forth as you walk, grasping its handle at your side. Or you may choose a papoose-style carrier or a stroller.

Going for a walk marks a big move toward independence, particularly if, unrestrained by parental hand, your 1-1/2-year-old can wander this way and that, searching for things to examine: a leaf, a stone, an insect, a bit of dirt too tiny to catch your glance. Your little one squats down, its diapered rear barely scraping the cement, and teetering on bended limbs, it closely examines a microscopic speck clutched between thumb and finger. Then, the subject closed, it rises effortlessly and scurries flat-footed down the forward path, seeking other sights.

Its limbs will grow strong with exercise, walking, running, dashing hither and yon. Then will come the next burst of increased freedom: Your child will get a tricycle or some other wheeled vehicle.

Your Child's First Wheels

Our family acquired a small tricycle, old and battered, the rubber tread gone from the left pedal. Each of our seven children learned to ride on it. Because it was small, they outgrew it after a year and graduated to a larger model, passing the smaller trike on to the next sibling. When our last child had outgrown it, we gave it to a neighbor at the campus where I taught. Some 15 years later, I saw a little boy—a stranger to me—peddling it on the sidewalk in front of his home. His parents had gotten it, with a lengthy series of family exchanges in-between, from our campus neighbor.

Eventually you are going to reach that critical time in your child's development when you have to ask yourself, "Is it time to buy the bike?" We're talking big-time wheels here—two-wheelers—not that kind of transition called "training-wheel time." Bicycles represent a step up in the world of freedom and mobility. With a bike, you can go on a trip. With a bike, you can fall and get hurt! So you pause and ask, "Is it time to buy the bike?" This is a watershed time for you. Your child sees it as just another time when you don't want it to do what it feels perfectly competent to do. You see it as possible injury for your child! Sooner or later, the die is cast. You buy a bike. Now begins the next traumatic stage for you: watching your child learn how to ride. You will begin the instruction, drawing upon your own foggy reminiscences of when you were a boy.

"Balance!" you emphasize. "The secret is in keeping your balance. Sit straight up and don't lean! Keep peddling unless you are going to stop." With that confusing flurry of commands, your child starts out. You hold the back of the seat firmly and begin to trot alongside as your child desperately peddles, its glazed eyes focused rigidly ahead. As the speed exceeds your trotting ability, you let go, praying fervently that you have not consigned your child to a suicidal course of action.

Once in a while, a child is able to ride the very

first try. Don't count on it being your child. More likely your little one will wobble down the sidewalk or driveway, missing obstacles by inches, bailing out onto the lawn head first just moments before disaster, leaving the bike to fend for itself.

You start the process again, and again, and again. Finally, your child continues on its way. The wobble corrects. The bike whizzes around the corner—its rider smiling triumphantly—out of sight!

"First-Bike" Decisions

There are a whole host of these "when-to-buy-the-bike" situations that will accent your relationship with your growing child. You will agonize as your infant struggles to lift its head to view its growing world, as it turns over for the first time, as it takes its first step, as it makes its first visit to a neighbor's house for lunch, or leaves for its first day at school, or takes its first driving lesson, starts its first job, goes out on its first date.

Each of these events represents a moment of danger and potential harm. And because you love your child, you are more acutely aware of this. Each also represents a little tug away from you, a little less dependence upon you, a bit more freedom and independence from you—and you will have mixed feelings about that.

We have to let our children go, have to let them

grow up and go away from us to be themselves. The problem always is—apart from our aching father heart—when and how much to let go.

We supervise our child's movement into the backyard or playground. We make the momentous decision when a sandbox is to be prepared. We secure a backyard pool, fill it with water, and hover about anxiously. We attempt to secure our power tools from curious childhood fingers, insulate all electrical implements against shock, gate all unprotected steps against wobbly walkers. Anxiously we watch our unstable little one negotiate a set of steps for the first time, then dash to the rescue as, fearlessly, it turns to make a grand descent.

The list of ways your untried child can hurt itself without your guiding hand grows. Yet you cannot hide it away, leave it locked up in infancy where it is safe and secure. Your child's heavenly Father has given it to the world to be a blessing in it and a blessing to it. Your child cannot do it if it is immature and tucked away. So help your child safely explore its world and find the pathways of opportunity God has laid out for it to follow as His child.

One of my twins was an inveterate "on-father's-lap" sitter. She fit there so perfectly, I suspected God had designed her for that very purpose. One day we were engaged in one of our very serious philosophic discussions.

The topic that day was growing up. She solemnly promised me, staring deep into my eyes, that, unlike her siblings, she was never going to grow up. She would always remain small enough to sit on my lap and keep me company. Last year I preached for her wedding, and as I watched her look into her husband's eyes, whispering, "I love you, Les!" I knew it was time to buy the bike—for the last time. Yet I wonder whether she will someday have a daughter. And that daughter will love her grandpa and, sooner or later, she will need a bike. And she will need someone to help her learn to ride.

The Art of Cheerleading

Almost 2,000 years ago, Paul, with his assistant Timothy, wrote a letter to the parishes of Phillipi, a city in what today is the country of Greece. He introduced the letter's close with these words:

"Always rejoice in the Lord. I'm going to say that again: Rejoice!"

Why do you suppose he felt the need to repeat himself? I suspect it may be because the Phillipians were not happy being the children of God. They were busy burdening themselves with spiritual duties. Perhaps they were afraid to trust God to take care of their future for them so they assumed the responsibility themselves.

The author of Psalm 118 states the familiar words, "This is the day the Lord has made. Let us rejoice and be glad in it!" Since he needed to encourage his readers to rejoice, it is apparent that Old Testament people also had difficulty rejoicing at being God's chosen people.

Rejoicing is a difficult habit to acquire. Acquiring it as a young child, when there is little empirical experience to frustrate it, helps. Therefore, you have yet another task as father: Teach your family how to rejoice in the Lord. With this task is the job of creating an environment of harmony and mutual love in which your family can take pleasure and easily rejoice in God.

Fostering Family Enjoyment

Your family's enjoyment begins, in many cases, with the mutual pleasure that your small child gives to you and your wife. As parents, enjoy and take pride in each little step of progress, recording for posterity by camera or camcorder every event in your young child's life. As time passes, however, relationships may grow strained.

The book of Genesis abounds with dysfunctional families, beginning with the first family where the anger of one son caused the death of his brother. Other examples follow in succeeding generations. Note how in the family of Isaac the roots of conflict are found in the biases of Rebecca and Isaac, each for a different twin son. That division carries over into the family of the younger son, Jacob, culminating in the slavery of Joseph in Egypt. Even in his final words to his sons, Jacob continues to sow the seeds of dissension among them. The patriarchs, whatever other virtues they may have had, were certainly not outstanding fathers.

Families that enjoy one another's company are easily detected. They seem to be comfortable with one another. They seem happy. Others are attracted to them. They are the ones to whose backyard children of the neighborhood gravitate, whether they have a plethora of toys or not. Toys may attract for a time, but they cannot compensate for an environment where children do not feel comfortable. As children grow older, children of God who are happy in their family tend to attract children who are not.

During the formative years, families that are creative and adventuresome need little other than their own ideas to find life together with God exciting. They do not need to buy their pleasures or hire others to supply them. As their circle of friendship grows, others outside their immediate family become occasional participants in family pleasures. Then evangelism activities naturally flow out of family outreach. Those who enjoy the company of this family share the source of their specialness in worship.

Rejoicing in Your Differences

One of the sources of family pleasure is the special difference of each member. Somehow, as the Spirit is at work, He brings out the unique talents and personality of each person. God loves individuals individually. He fosters and coaxes out each one's uniqueness.

When my children were growing, I impressed upon each that they were special because they were children of God and that each had his or her unique way of being. One of them took to referring to herself as "Dad's Special Person." All my children took pride in that uniqueness and, at the same time, in being a member of our family. I marvel that, to the best of my knowledge, none ever became conceited, but each, from personal and familial security, enjoyed contributing to their world in a quiet and unassuming way.

Treasuring the Moments

During the years to come you will have many days of family rejoicing—special days, trips together, outings, graduations, weddings. Objects of childhood will collect and move to the attic, forgotten, even as their memory moves to the back of your mind. Years from now, perhaps as you break up housekeeping, you will come upon those dusty childhood treasures and relive those days.

So also the treasures of daily family rejoicing, those anticipations and reflections that bring delight to each day, are stored in our attic memory. There they remain until, years later, we take them from their respective hiding places, dust them off, and treasure them again. Sometimes the fondness of these memories is tinged by the bittersweet background of a parental death. As children distribute amongst themselves the remnants of their parents' lives, no father or mother remains to thank for golden days of which these trinkets are at best a vestige of the wondrous past. It was good, being your child!

Father, Ph.D.

Your child's formative years will be undergirded by its mistaken belief that you know everything. Your child will implicitly trust you and your wife in everything, unless given good reason not to. Even when your feet of clay are painfully exposed, your child will continue to come to you with questions.

As soon as your child can talk, it will ask you questions, some of which you can easily answer, and some of which are simply unanswerable, such as, "How far does *up* go?"

Parents as Educators

Until it begins its years of formal education, you and your wife are your child's primary educators. Thereafter, you have a few more years before your child concludes that its teacher knows more than you do and will attempt to correct you, quoting the teacher. Until that time comes, there are at least three things you need to keep in mind.

- The question your child is asking is not necessarily the question it wants answered.

- Your child may learn more from what you do than from what you say.
- You are your child's primary resource for filling out the spiritual dimension of reality because you are its God surrogate.

What's the Question?

Children are sometimes very direct in their questioning, in particular with respect to specifics. They are not very good in framing questions about general and more philosophic matters. They will frame their questions in the simple language that they possess, somewhat like attempting to solve all mathematical problems with simple arithmetic operations.

The secret to successfully answering a question may very well lie in helping a child more clearly explain what the problem is or helping it rephrase its question. Finding out why a question is being asked is often helpful, particularly with a young child. Often in the process of being questioned, your child may very well figure out for itself the answer it has been seeking. One of the rules of good education is: Never answer a question your child can figure out for itself. Instead, teach it how to figure out the answers.

When your 3-year-old asks you a simple question, how you deal with that question will affect, in a minor way, how it directs its future pursuit of knowledge. We sometimes think that education consists of filling children's memories with the answers to a whole host of questions. This may equip them to win prizes on quiz shows; it does not prepare them for life. Given the plethora of new information flooding our world and the rapid degree of change, children need tools for discovering and evaluating information, not bodies of information to absorb.

A small child needs to accumulate a basic store of information that it will supplement and revise through life. At least at the start, you may get a whole host of "What-is-this?" questions that call for direct answers. At the same time, a small child has a brief span of interest, within which your answer will have to fit or it will lose interest and move to something else.

How Did You Do That?

Your child, without thinking, will copy you much more than you realize, particularly if it's a boy. The same is true with daughters and their mothers. You are already familiar with your child's assigning to God some of your behavioral characteristics; it will also spontaneously reflect your mannerisms in its own behavior. Your child may start to walk like you. Certainly it will start to talk like you, use your inflections, cadences, and rate of speaking. It will begin to use your language, including some expressions you may not want to hear. You will certainly want to hear the God you love addressed and spoken of with affection by your child. That will not always be the case, maybe because it is not always the case with you.

What Does God Expect of Me?

God reduced how He wished us to treat Him and one another to 10 commands. Have you ever wondered, given the small number of commands He chose to use, that one had to do with the appropriate use of His name? Given that importance, one of your most significant educational tasks will be to help your child become skillful in addressing and discussing its heavenly Father.

Another task concerns the habit of worship. Another will concern your child's relation to you, your wife, and its brothers and sisters. As it gets older, you will have to address the subjects of the later commands: bodily harm, abuse of sex, theft, false witness, and covetousness. Remember, you and your wife are the primary educators regarding these subjects.

Whether you make a conscious effort or not, your child will absorb its values from you. If you are abusive to others, your child will likely have little concern for others' physical well-being. If you engage in illicit sex or condone it, your child will likely grow up to exhibit similar behavior and attitudes. If you do not teach it to recognize and respect property lines and rights, your child will assume that whatever is accessible to it is usable by it, regardless of ownership. If it does not learn the virtue of honesty and integrity, you may find yourself some day with a devious child. And if you envy your neighbor his or her good fortune, you may some day live to regret a covetous and discontented child.

Formal Education

Sooner or later you begin to share the task of your child's education with others. First, perhaps, may be the Sunday school or the preschool teacher. Then your child will embark upon the long years of formal education from which it will emerge at some level, hopefully prepared to take its place among its fellow citizens as a useful member of society.

You dare never lose sight of the larger picture and the greater goal for which formal education is but a small part. Our Lord Jesus Christ, on the night He was betrayed, told His disciples, "I am the Way, the Truth, and the Life." Anything that is true—right up to the way we are rescued from sin and saved for eternal life—in some way or other is about Him. If your child is to keep living as His child, it needs to become increasingly sensitive through life to the presence of its Lord Jesus Christ in its heart. It needs to be able to sort out the urges that come from God from those that do not, to recognize opportunities He provides for greater service to Him. Your child can even learn to recognize that failures and disappointments can be woven into a life of service to God as He uses these means to change the momentum, direction, or focus of life. Regardless of whatever else educators may be doing for your child, your task remains as primary educator.

13
Assistant Alter Ego

Your small child will spend a great deal of time examining all sorts of things, including, after a little time, its own body. This discovery may come at the expense of some pain: scratching itself, poking itself in the eye with a finger, biting a toe. When it gets a bit older, it will be curious about other children, particularly children of the other gender. It will be incapable of examining its inner life and evaluating its thoughts and behavior until it is older, at the time when its conscience emerges as a sort of alter ego.

About the age of 3 or 4, children have developed enough of an inner reality, and are aware of themselves as persons enough, to begin feeling conflict in the form of shame. Perhaps with that self-awareness comes an unconscious awareness of human sinfulness as they, like their primal parents, seek to hide themselves from others.

Though your young child is capable of feeling ashamed, it is not yet capable of feeling guilty. The conscience, which is the source of that feeling, will not emerge as a functioning ethical resource until about age 10. From that time on, if all has developed normally, conscience will act as an alter ego within the child's self-awareness, criticizing its thoughts and behavior. Until that time, you have to function as an assistant alter ego, hence the title of this chapter.

Consciences are inner warning systems and inner judicial systems, "buzzing" when we are thinking of doing something we believe is against the will of God, and giving us massive guilt feelings when we think we have done wrong. Because they function in those fashions, we need to have our systems functioning properly, or we will end up with a lot of grief and not much use from our conscience.

Molding Your Child's Conscience

Consciences do not just suddenly emerge, functioning perfectly. Sometimes, for one reason or other, they do not emerge at all. A person without conscience is amoral, lacking any sensitivity to right and wrong. Sometimes conscience emerges warped, having peculiar ways of responding to the behavior of its possessor. To avoid these results, from rebirth in Baptism your child's conscience has to be molded. Then, at the appropriate time, it will emerge in such condition that your child will be able to use it to assist its service to God.

Initially, as far as your child is concerned, what God wants and what you want are identical. You will teach by approving and disapproving of your child's behavior. It will learn what you like and what you do not like. Since it will automatically transfer your values to its understanding of God, they will become a part of the content of its conscience or reinforce what is already there.

During its childhood, you can next begin to explain how God wants your child to live and, when it acts contrary to what God wants, explain how and why what it did was displeasing to Him. The task is not as difficult as it might seem because you already have two things working in your favor: Your child is already rightly motivated because God lives in its heart, and your child has the law of God already there in its nature, albeit defectively because of its sinfulness. Later, when your child can reflect on its actions, you can help it recognize motivations that are from God and distinguish them from those that are not.

As your child grows older and attends Sunday school, you may explicitly talk about what Jesus likes or doesn't like. If your child is unusually reflective, it may ask questions or, if independent, may well challenge what it is taught. Thus, the content form of its conscience will grow and be shaped.

Being Your Child's Conscience

Until your child's conscience emerges, you need to be its conscience. Therefore, you have to be careful not to alienate your child from you. I suspect this is part of what the prophet meant when he said, "And you fathers, provoke not your children to wrath, but bring them up in the nurture and admonition of God."

In rearing your child, you will need to avoid two mistakes. The one is assuming that your child has only a divine nature. You raise your child nondirectively, allowing it to do as it pleases, assuming it will unerringly discover the will of God. This approach may not only produce a neighborhood social monster, it will contribute nothing to the formation of your child's conscience.

The other error is assuming your child has only a demonic nature. You criticize virtually everything your child does, lest it grow up a bad boy or girl. You fail to recognize the presence of your child's spiritual nature and do nothing to foster it since all your measures are repressive. As a result, your child will either become neurotic, lacking confidence in itself to do any good, or its nature as a child of God will be crushed. It will rebel against you and God or hypocritically obey you until it is old enough to escape. You need to be even-handed in dealing with your child's dual nature, praising that which is pleasing to God and seeking, appropriately, to repress that which is not good.

As your child's world grows, it will encounter competing values. If you have done your job well, competing values will be resisted or will be tested against those your child has gained from you. Not until its conscience has been at work for a decade are your values and the content of its conscience likely to be subjected to general critical review.

Ironing Out the Discrepancies

You undoubtedly will find that biases begin to emerge in your child's values. Perhaps they were implicit in your own, emerging in mirror form in your child's self-expression. You may have times of confrontation as you criticize your child's behavior and it offers your own past behavior as the model. You may find your upper-grade child coming home from school, or a party, or a visit to another church espousing values that you cannot approve. All of these are evidence that, as consciences are forming, they can err over a wide range of values. You need to be careful, therefore, to bring your child's values back into conformity with the will of God in order that its conscience will be a faithful instrument.

As you find your young child floundering in its attempts to please you and God amidst an overwhelming flood of "dos" and "don'ts," pause periodically to hug and kiss it, assure it of your approval, and disentangle it from the web of laws that have developed to strangle it. Above all, don't try to direct your relationships or your home by dispassionate law.

On Mount Sinai, God thundered, "Remember the Sabbath Day to keep it holy!" In Galilee, in the grain fields, the Son of God said, gently, "The Sabbath was made for men, not man for the Sabbath." In these words, we see the function and limit of law. It is ever a means to something greater than itself and never an end in itself. As you teach your child, giving it rules or laying down laws, do it in such a way that your child knows why such regulation is good.

Family Confession

We cannot conclude the subject of this chapter without returning to the subject of confession. In the Middle Ages, religious community members lived in close proximity to one another. They found that, to preserve the group spirituality, they needed a time for individual daily confession, either to the community or to the head of the order, whereafter they were absolved of their sin.

Your family can be a similar community. You don't need time for daily individual confession and absolution, but periodically, even the best of families need to cleanse themselves and begin afresh, forgiven and reconciled to one another. Such times are best begun when you, the head of the household, confess your weaknesses and shortcomings and beg the forgiveness of the family.

There was a time when the model of parenthood was patterned after "father-knows-best" TV shows. We seem to have slipped from that stereotype into another, a sort of Dagwood Bumstead model: "Father is a dolt, but he has a smart wife." Neither is accurate. We all, even the best of us, make mistakes, lose our tempers, hurt the ones we love, and need to be forgiven by them.

If you can establish a confessional family, you will find that each of you is easier and more open with one another. None has any secret sins that he or she is hiding. Confession and forgiveness flow freely, and each person is concerned not to hurt the other. Yours will be a healthier and happier family.

WHEN ALL OF YOU ARE HURTING

Every family encounters crises: sickness, accidents, death, financial reverses, external or internal hostilities, fire, natural disasters, etc.—unexpected reversals that affect a family's happiness. Some families plan for them, practicing home evacuation in case of a fire, basement sheltering in case of a tornado, or handling home invasion by a robber. They may have instructions about medications: what to do in case of accidental poisoning, or falling down and getting a scrape, or breaking a bone. Children may be taught how to summon help by telephone and state their name and address and whatever other information outside help might need. When an emergency occurs, they know who is in charge and what to do.

Sometimes instruction yields unusual results.

My wife and I returned from shopping one day to find our son hovering anxiously at the side of one of our daughters who was lying down on the living room sofa, a towel firmly bound to the top of her head. He informed us that while playing in the backyard, she had been accidentally struck by a toy thrown by one playmate to another. As a result, she had received a nasty cut on the top of her head, the bleeding of which he was stanching with a turkish towel. Complimenting him on his quick action, I removed the towel to determine whether the cut warranted a trip to the hospital emergency room. As the towel came away, I was struck by an unexpected but familiar smell. Proudly he informed me that he had protected the wound with the only antiseptic he could find, the last few ounces of a bottle of 12-year-old Scotch.

Crises draw a family together, teach them the importance of praying for one another, and increase their dependency upon God and upon one another. When a child has been gravely injured or ill and returns home restored to health, that child gains new value to the family as they realize what it would be like without it. When one member dies, the family learns to grieve together and tries to stitch up the hole left by that missing one. When the family suffers together in a crisis, petty quarrels and rivalries are forgotten. Children gain new understanding and appreciation for one another as, forgetting themselves, they protect others in the family. Once, while hiking along a wooded mountain trail, I slipped over the side and slid down about 10 feet. Instantly my son was at my side with the anxious words, "Are you okay, Dad?"

Surviving Childhood Illness

Sooner or later crises arise in every family. Many of these crises will involve illness. Small children can develop sudden high fevers. Their eyes burning with fever, they look pleadingly at you to make them better. You pray. You hold them close in your arms like one of the ancient prophets and plead with God for their life. You try to infuse their burning body by a sheer act of will with some of your healthy vitality. You bathe them with a cold cloth to draw off some of the heat or try to coax them into swallowing a little cool water. In such moments, you feel your total helplessness and remember all the times you could have enjoyed or given pleasure to this little one—but you were always too busy. And then—as suddenly as it began—the fever passes. Everything returns to normal—including, perhaps, your normal busyness.

Your child will have most of the childhood illnesses for which we have developed no immunities. Thank God your child is spared the likelihood of infant mortality, diphtheria, polio, and some of the other illnesses that used to take an annual toll of children. You can prepare your child for times of childhood illness with a special prayer like the one I learned when I was about 3, sick with whooping cough.

Tender Jesus, meek and mild,
Look on me your little child.
Help me if it is your will
To recover from my ill.
Amen.

Needless to say, my children also learned the prayer. Feel free to teach it to your children, one of a number of set prayers they can learn for various special occasions.

Taking the Fear Out of the Word *Hospital*

I do not know what the ratio is between the number of children in a family and the number of trips to the hospital to set a broken bone. I suspect it is on the order of four to one. The more children you have, the more likely an injury requiring a hospital visit, and perhaps a hospital stay. The anticipation of a hospital stay is frightening for anyone—especially for a small child. Children often get the idea that hospitals are places one goes to die, and they are afraid when they learn they have to go to the hospital.

If you can retain your calm in anticipating such a visit, your child will respond. I have found 1 Peter 5:7 useful in such times of tension: "Cast all your anxiety on him because he cares for you." Recognizing your child's fear, hold its hands to pray about that fear to its heavenly Father. Hug your small child yourself as it lets go of the fears, perhaps with a burst of tears. It's therapeutic. The faith feeling that follows, as one simply trusts God to do everything, can be as exhilarating as a roller coaster ride. Trusting God will come more easily for your child than for you. Your child has the word of its father that God will do what is best.

When Your Child Pushes You Away

Thoughts of illness, disease, and death are far from your mind, of course, as you await your child's birth or hold your newly-baptized infant. That little one will give you years of incredible joy. However, it may, with little advance warning, begin to exhibit hostility and alienate itself from you. Any number of causes may produce the behavior: the influence of a school friend who is hostile to its parents, some disagreement with you that resulted in treatment it resents, some action unknown to you about which it feels guilty, the early stages of a mental difficulty, your clumsiness in approaching a matter on which it is sensitive, or simply some irrational impulse that continues until it gets out of hand.

In such situations, it is easy to adopt the "blameless-superior-father" approach—guaranteed not to work! You need to emulate our loving God at His touching best. Show your child that you care—search for it and and let it see your suffering. If you want to win back your child, you have to endure its self-protective defenses until you can discover the cause of its alienation and remove it. You have to wade between its flailing fists in order to draw it close to you to hug it.

In a second sense, you have to reveal to your child the pain you are feeling. Nothing dissolves a child's hostility faster than the discovery that the parent, thought to be cold and indifferent, is deeply troubled and pained by the child's blind hatred. If you show your pain, your child may well be moved to reveal its own. Together you can ask our suffering Lord for mutual healing. The experience will leave a scar. A scar, however, is a place of former injury where the bond is now stronger than ever.

Crisis times show us how strong we have fashioned our familial bonds and how firmly we have lashed one another to the love of our Lord Jesus Christ. Crises are painful for us to endure. Under the healing influence of God the Holy Spirit, however, they remind us of the blessing that each of us is to the other.

A Father's Father

If being a father were simply a matter of asking your father what to do, books like this would not be written. Certainly there will be times when your father is a valuable expert to consult, but you will find that your times are far different from his, even as his times differed from his father's.

The Grandfather's Duties

As grandfather of your child, your father (and father-in-law) partake in activities that are much more precious, much more pleasant, and much more rewarding than second guessing you as you struggle with parental responsibilities. Your father knows something you will never know: what the world was like before you were born. He put in at least two decades in this world before you came along and then another half decade before the two of you had much of any accumulated personal history. It's all there, in his memory, waiting to be shared with your child.

Between your father's birth and your child's birth stretches a half-century, a large part of which he can personalize by giving it to your child in the form of reminiscences. He is your family's patriarch, the keeper of the flame, the preserver of the traditions, the one who has the experience and the wisdom to define the unique character of those who possess your name.

That may not mean much to you as you are starting out as a father. The duties of today and the bills of tomorrow loom much greater in your consciousness than your father's boyhood memories and the great historic times through which he lived. But if your father is like the one that I have described, then you will soon want your little ones to get to know your dad as a personal historian and to learn from him as much as they can while he is still available.

Listening at Grandpa's Knee

We Americans, with our restless ways and eager desire to change and forge ahead, suffer by comparison with peoples of ancient cultures who move through life at a more leisurely pace, pausing regularly to savor the goodness of their past. As more and more of our grandfathers live on after retirement, they have time to reflect upon and digest the family saga, integrating their past with that of their parents and grandparents in order to pass it on to their grandchildren.

One of the vivid memories of my boyhood finds its setting in the front room of my father's parents. Along one wall, over the upright piano, two large pictures hung, each a foot-and-a-half by two feet, framed in 19th-century frames. Brought over from Germany by my grandfather, they were his father and his mother, sober and severe in their demeanor. They were his tie to the family in the "old country" which he had left in his early 20s to escape another of the Kaiser's wars.

He never told me about them, my great-grandparents, other than that they lived in Potzdam on the Hohenzoellern estate, Castle San Souci. My father and I were named after that great-grandfather. I wish he had said more. I know my grandfather was one of two brothers, and his brother had only girls so my grandfather carried on the family name alone. When my maiden aunt broke up housekeeping after the death of my widowed grandmother, she gave those pictures to me. They hung over the piano in my front room for better than 30 years. Today, in my retirement, they hang in my son's front room, over the piano. Some day they will belong to my grandson.

Putting Time to Good Use

Grandparents, unlike anyone else, have the privilege to be pure gospel people. They can love the daylights out of their grandchildren and never have to tell them no! Children need older adults with whom to exchange affection with complete trust, who will listen to them uncritically, on their own level, person to person, as long as they want to converse. Grandparents have a lot of time when they have retired. No one is waiting to hear what they have to say; they have no subordinates who stand in awe of them; they don't have to prove anything to anyone; they've probably already achieved whatever they are going to achieve, so far as this world is concerned, so they can concentrate on just caring for their grandchildren.

The Family Network

The word *network* has become popular in recent years. Large families had networks long before the term was invented. They tended to center upon the grandparents, then branch out like spokes from a hub to every child's family, like satellites of the center. Even today, married children of a loving family, unless they live near one another, tend to communicate with one another through the parental home. Grandma and Grandpa often know more than anyone else what is going on here and there in the relation. They pass on the news as they see fit. So, they keep the family together though they are apart.

That role lies far down the road for you as you

anticipate, or begin to raise, your first child. Watch your father as he begins to relate to your offspring. If you and your dad have never been close, you may find that your child brings you together as you see how his eyes light up at the sight of his grandchild. He will always care how your child is doing, lending a listening ear, not only to share your joy at your child's achievements but to comfort you and give a sage word of wisdom when there are problems. He will also comfort and console your wife, holding her in his fatherly arms when you have problems too great for the two of you to bear alone or when fear or grief have frozen your hearts. Your father's playing god for you does not end just because you have children of your own.

THE BOTTOM LINE

As a good father, you probably have some concern about what this enterprise called "Being a Father" is going to cost. You already suspect that it will require an investment of much longer duration than becoming a car owner or a home owner. Unlike either of those items, a child can't be traded in on a newer model (there was a time when we said that also about spouses) or fixed like new if you damage it. Even if you trade it to another father, it will still remain connected emotionally to you, child to father and father to child.

Adding Up the Financial Cost

The dollar cost is most easily calculated. The financial cost of child maintenance increases from birth until high school, accelerates dramatically during the high school years, and if the child attends college, skyrockets almost beyond your means. Thereafter, the costs decline just as precipitously unless the child is female, in which case there will be one more drain on the family purse for the wedding to which she and her mother think she is entitled. After that, except for an occasional loan, all the costs are for gifts at birthday times and Christmas for them and their progeny. If your child happens to be developmentally limited, however, he or she will be a lifelong financial concern, although some governmental agencies will probably help you with costs and services.

By another measurement, a family of any size will wear out one set of household furnishings, two or three cars, one lawn, several sets of carpeting, three or four sets of dishes, and the interior of one entire house. Once the brood has taken off, most of the old family home will likely need refurbishing and modernizing. In spite of the objections of your offspring, the family home should probably be sold because, with only you and your wife left, the place is far too large; the lawn is too much for an aging parent to mow; and the necessity, to say nothing of the urge, to have a big vegetable garden has long since disappeared. On the other hand, careful real estate swapping may return a generous profit for your retirement fund.

Adding Up the Emotional and Spiritual Cost

Sizeable as financial outlays may be for each child, much more sizeable is the investment of:

>time,
>>worry,
>>>concern,
>>>>prayer,
>>>>>advising children who listen with half an ear, trying to talk a stubborn offspring out of a hair-brained idea,
>>>>>>tears, and
>>>>>>>the general wear and tear on the nerves

that each child in its own way costs a father who is trying his best to do a good job. These costs far outweigh the monetary.

Added to that is the fact that often children will be totally insensitive to their parents' feelings. They sometimes accept parental gifts, for which those parents have sacrificed, as though the United States Constitution and the Bill of Rights guarantee them as their inalienable right.

Children can be rude. They can be nasty. They can be intolerant. They can be as impossible as they think their father is. And you can't unload them on somebody else's front step in a basket some dark and foggy night. Your daughter may marry some lout who hates even to see you, much less address you as "Dad," so you seldom see your child whom you raised. He gets all the benefit without paying anything for the privilege.

The Reality of Fatherhood

You will not produce perfect offspring. The real world is far different from the world of the baby books and the "father-knows-best" TV shows.

On the other hand, let's look at this business of being a father long-term, in the bright light of eternity.

- *Every time you have a child, you have produced someone who is intended by God to live in heaven forever.* You get a chance to work with the Holy Spirit for a few years to get that person ready for active and productive kingdom work. Regardless of what the evangelism people tell you, the primary mission field of the church is the marriage bed, the place where most of the church of tomorrow gets its start, not in door-to-door calling, mass mailings, or radio or television broadcasts. Procreation builds the body of Christ.

- *Second, every time you get a child from God the Father, you have an opportunity to give it right back to Him, like Hannah.* When my son, who is my oldest child, was born, he was baptized in my father's church. In return for baptizing him there, I preached the sermon that day. It was on the Hannah text: giving our children to the Lord. My son happened to feel called to study for the ministry and did. When his son was born, he baptized him and preached on the same Hannah text.

Your child doesn't have to become a professional church worker to be given to the Lord. When you give that child to God in Baptism and thereafter, raise it as a father surrogate for God, regardless of what profession it enters, you give it to God.

- *Third, if you work it right, you are going to get a lot of love in return, certainly a great deal more than you deserve.* That love continues on through life. Last night, one of my daughters called me to wish me a belated happy birthday. We talked for half-an-hour on her nickel, neither one wanting to say goodbye, each feeling the love that binds us together—the telephone company made a tremendous profit from our affection. (My wife and I own telephone stock in self-defense.) Love like that is not available for sale anywhere. You build it together over the decades.

- *Fourth, if you have done it right, there will always be at least someone who thinks you are the greatest person there is in the whole world.* It's not your wife. She knows well enough from personal experience all your limitations. The Word of God promises you that your sons and daughters will rise up to praise you in your old age. No one can put a price on that. It can't be bought. I feel sorry for people I know who, from choice, have no children. No one is there who loves them as they get old, no one who looks up to them, no one who cares. In their loneliness they age, surrounded by the possessions for which they sacrificed a family.

My mother is 92. Her body is fragile and stiff, her mind sharp as a tack. She bore and raised eight children. She doesn't own a house. Never has. She doesn't drive a car. Never has. She has album after album of family pictures, memories, and stories for her children. She gets letters and phone calls from her children, her grandchildren, and her great-grandchildren. She is the family librarian; she knows what everyone is doing. Her grandchildren make special trips to see her, regardless of where they live, to show her their children. She is the richest woman I know although she subsists on Social Security and the pension of a pastor's widow.

- *Fifth, when you've been a caring father, your children and your grandchildren will care for you in that same way.* I acknowledge that grandmothers tend to get priority treatment, especially from their grandsons, but there is plenty of affection left for grandfathers, crotchety as they might get sometimes.

"They shall rise up and honor the face of the old man." You have to get a lot of years behind you to appreciate what that means. I'm still adjusting to the "sirs" I get from my students or how they adjust their pace to match my slower step. My children do their best, unobtrusively, to look out for me when we go climbing in the mountains or play golf, adjusting their step or wanting to stop for a moment, now and then, to admire the view—to let me catch my breath.

- *Sixth, when you are a father, there is always someone who needs you.* Even after the years of financial dependency, your children will continue to need you, to check in with you periodically, to let you know how they are doing and what they have achieved. They want their friends to meet you, and they want to meet their friends' dads. It is important to be wanted. When in a sour mood, it helps to have a child sit you down to explain what you have meant and what you mean for them, just being there. You taught them that a family costs a lot of money but is worth many times over what it costs. They will teach you that a good father is priceless—even if he doesn't have a dime—if he loves his children.

- *Finally, your children are your investment in the future and in eternity.* Unlike other investments, you can take with you what you gave them and what they gave you because you gave them the love of their Lord Jesus Christ and they gave Him back to you in an infinite number of little ways.

CEOs try to set up golden parachutes to float them gently to the ground when they are fired. The best of fathers send aloft golden balloons, inflated by their children's love, to lift them over the hard places of old age and float them into eternity. Thus, buoyed up by their offsprings' ascendant prayers to the throne of God, fathers make their quiet hiatus from this present time. They grasp the hand of God even as they relax their human hand, weathered and worn, cradled in the weeping grasp of those whom from infancy they have loved.

The Lord keep you! Have a blessed fatherhood!